A Confidential Matter

The Letters of Richard Strauss and Stefan Zweig, 1931–1935

Max Knight is the author of *Return to the Alps* and other works. Among his many translations are *The Pure Theory of Law* by Hans Kelsen, and works by Morgenstern, Brecht, Heine, and Karl Kraus.

Stefan Zweig

A Confidential Matter

The Letters of Richard Strauss and Stefan Zweig, 1931–1935

Translated from the German by Max Knight
Foreword by Edward E. Lowinsky

UNIVERSITY OF CALIFORNIA PRESS

Berkeley / Los Angeles / London

Translated, with permission, from
Richard Strauss/Stefan Zweig: Briefwechsel,
edited by Willi Schuh. Frankfurt am Main:
S. Fischer Verlag, 1957.

University of California Press
Berkeley and Los Angeles, California

University of California Press, Ltd.
London, England

ISBN 0-520-03036-2
Library of Congress Catalog Card Number: 75-13162
Printed in the United States of America

Contents

Translator's Note

To make the political and to some extent also the literary background more accessible to the American reader, I have added footnotes and also minor interpolations [indicated by square brackets] in the text and in the backnotes provided by the editor of the German edition. For help in these emendations and for saving me from errors by reading the manuscript, I am indebted to several friends whose kindness I wish to acknowledge: Robert Breuer (New York), Professor Edward E. Lowinsky (University of Chicago and Milan), Professor Peter Paret (Stanford University), Willi Schuh (Zurich), William Steinberg (Pittsburgh, Palo Alto), William and Leila Vennewitz (Vancouver), Professor Harry Zohn (Brandeis University), and my perceptive colleague Doris Kretschmer.

The photograph of Zweig was taken by Susanne B. Hoeller.

The original letters of Stefan Zweig to Richard Strauss are deposited at the Richard Strauss-Archiv in Garmisch, the original letters of Richard Strauss to Stefan Zweig at the library of the State University of New York at Fredonia.

M. K.

Foreword

The correspondence between Stefan Zweig and Richard Strauss is one of the most intensely interesting documents of our time. It reads like a drama. Strauss, in fifty years of search, had found only one poet capable of writing the librettos that his specific musical talent and temperament required, Hugo von Hofmannsthal. When Hofmannsthal died in 1929, Strauss was convinced it was all over with his work as opera composer.

In 1931 Strauss asked a common friend to sound out Stefan Zweig whether he might be willing to write a libretto for him, and thus a fateful concatenation of events was set in motion that led to the creation of *Die schweigsame Frau* and to a human and artistic relationship of the most intimate kind, more and more overshadowed by the political events of the years 1933–35, when the correspondence comes to a rather sudden and entirely unpredictable end.

Strauss was well aware of Stefan Zweig's consuming love for music. The poet's collection of autographs of writers and musicians. was internationally known. It contained a Bach cantata, arias by Gluck and Handel, Mozart's "Das Veilchen," Cherubino's aria from *Figaro*, Beethoven's "Der Kuss" and fragments of the music for *Egmont*, Schubert's "An die Musik," Chopin's *Barcarole*, Brahms' *Zigeunerlieder*. Undoubtedly, Strauss knew the six songs of Max Reger set to texts from the first book of poems *(Silberne Saiten)* of the nineteen-year-old Zweig.[1]

---

1. What Strauss did not know and Zweig himself appears to have forgotten—at any rate it is not mentioned in his autobiography—is that at the age of twenty-six while sending Reger a new book of poems, he offered him also an opera libretto (Arens, 190; facsimile of Reger's letter on pp. 110–11), to which

The correspondence opens with a letter from Zweig's pen that reads almost like Tatiana's letter to the Prince in Pushkin's verse drama, *Eugene Onegin*: the famous writer addresses the older composer like a shy young girl a great man whom she has silently worshipped for years—except that in this case the older partner enthusiastically accepts the shy suitor. In his answer, Strauss, always uninhibited and direct, comes right to the point. He wants a libretto from Stefan Zweig. He tells him that in the center of that libretto ought to stand the type of woman not yet represented in his operas, the *grande dame* as international spy or the woman as racketeer. Hofmannsthal had not believed that it was still possible to write an intrigue play of wit and verve. Strauss wanted to begin with Zweig just where he had left off with Hofmannsthal.

The correspondence now developing is fascinating in a number of ways: as an exchange between two highly gifted, intelligent, articulate, and well-read artists; as a study in contrasts between two entirely different characters and temperaments, an infinitely sensitive, tactful, retiring, but brilliant writer, and a man overflowing with vitality, forthwright to the point of bluntness, almost coarse at times; as a school of enlightenment on the interaction between a composer and his librettist—in this respect the equal of the Strauss-Hofmannsthal correspondence—and in the end as a portrait of two intellectuals trying to cope with the Nazi regime. The political innocence of both Zweig and Strauss seems almost unbelievable. Both were convinced that things would simmer down after a while: Zweig sought refuge in a principled apolitical stance, Strauss in an entirely unprincipled, pragmatic belief that he could bend the regime to his purposes.

To begin with, they had to agree on a topic. After several proposals—among them a *grand ballet* that Zweig had conceived ten years before, thinking already then of Strauss—the poet suggests a comedy after Ben Jonson's *Epicoene, or The Silent Woman*. The composer accepts with relish and asks for a draft.

Reger responded with "highest interest," adding however: "whether I—absolute musician that I am—will ever write an opera I doubt very much." He never did.

When Zweig sends him the first outline, Strauss responds with an
enthusiasm that must have overwhelmed him: ". . . enchanting—
a born comic opera—a comedy equal to the best of its kind—
more suitable for music than even *Figaro* or the *Barber of Seville*"
(June 24, 1932). Two weeks after the outline was finished, Zweig
sends Strauss the first act and Strauss answers with a quote from
Die Meistersinger: "der erste Bar gelang." In response to the
second act comes a more cordial salute still, the initial measures of
Strauss's *Lied*: "Ach, dass ich dich gefunden, du liebes Kind!"
Strauss knew how to woo his newly found librettist. Zweig confesses
the composer's enthusiasm made the collaboration "an inde-
scribable pleasure" (*Welt*, 338), and Strauss, in his notes on "The
History of *Die schweigsame Frau*" (see Appendix, below), says:
"None of my earlier operas was so easy to compose, or gave me
such light-hearted pleasure."

So the libretto for *Die schweigsame Frau* was born. The miracle
that Strauss had given up hoping for materialized before his
astonished eyes: again he had found a partner, fully his equal,
and the equal of Hofmannsthal in ingenuity, wit, dramatic sense,
and literary genius. To have found him was good fortune. To
hold him, he naïvely believed, was up to himself.

Strauss's naïveté receives its first shock when he tries to persuade
Zweig to keep on writing for him, the political circumstances
notwithstanding. Goebbels, he claims, is on his side (February 26,
1935). Zweig does not believe it. Strauss decides to take the bull by
the horns. He speaks to Goebbels and his deputy minister about
the matter and is stunned when both men decline to take the
responsibility for a second Zweig-Strauss opera. Tongue in cheek,
he proposes a national contest for an opera libretto. In writing
to Zweig, he adds sardonically: "God have mercy on the Herr
Minister if he then has to read all those submitted texts!" The
contest never materialized (February 26, 1935).

In his autobiography, *Die Welt von Gestern*, Zweig, who had
many friends in Germany and many sources of information, reveals
what went on behind the stage. The performance of an opera
whose libretto was written by a Jew was becoming an affair of state

occupying innumerable officials. Zweig's discretion was the despair of the Ministry of Propaganda. If only he would commit a *faux pas*—from the regime's point of view—one could then rid oneself of him as an enemy of the German people. Failing this, his libretto was examined by all conceivable offices and persons, his books rummaged through for anti-German utterances. But Zweig, a passionate European, did not write against any nation.

In the beginning of the year 1934, the full score, the piano score, and the libretto were already in print. The Dresden Opera had ordered the costumes, the roles had been assigned. But the various spheres of power and jurisdiction, from Göring and Goebbels to Streicher, the most notorious Jew baiter among the Nazis, from the Kulturrat to the Reichsschrifttumskammer and the Ministry of Education, were unable to arrive at a solution to the problem. To perform a work in which a Jewish author had collaborated in any form at all was against the law put on the books as early as 1933. No office, no person would take the responsibility. Nothing would do but to submit the matter to Hitler in person. Goebbels advised Strauss to send his score to Hitler; on the next day he reduced the demand to the libretto. The "Führer" found the task not to his liking. One conference was called after another. Eventually, Strauss was cited before the all-powerful and in personal audience was informed that the performance of his opera, although contravening every law of the new Germany, would be permitted as a matter of special exception (*Welt*, 340–42).

In the meantime, Zweig was growing increasingly pessimistic about the survival of intellectual and artistic freedom in Germany. In a letter of August 27, 1934 to René Schickele, writer and companion of Romain Rolland, Zweig, and other pacifists, he had still expressed his belief that the Germans and Italians would rise up against tyranny (Prater, 229). But the events in Germany, in particular the Hindemith-Furtwängler affair at the end of the year 1934, cured him of such optimism. Hindemith, the uncontested leader of the younger generation of German composers, although a conservative among the moderns, was in the eyes of the

Nazis a "Kulturbolschewist," a "standard bearer of decadence."
His festivals of contemporary chamber music in Donaueschingen
were regarded by the Nazis as no less reprehensible than the artists
that Walter Gropius had assembled in the Bauhaus at Weimar.
Both institutions and their leaders were officially proscribed.

Hindemith's older counterpart, Arnold Schönberg, Austrian
Jew, leader of the school of "atonal" composers and the real radical,
had been recipient of the Liszt prize in Berlin, as a young
composer, upon recommendation of Richard Strauss. In the
year 1925 he was called to Berlin to head a master class in composition at the Preussische Akademie der Künste. Now he was
dismissed without ceremony or right of appeal. The letter of
dismissal was signed in May 1933 by the composer and conductor
Max von Schillings, who, in 1932, had succeeded as President of
the Academy of Arts Max Liebermann, leading German
painter, a native of Berlin, and a Jew. Not one voice rose in protest
from the ranks of German composers, musicians, intellectuals—
a signal to the regime that they could proceed with their plans.
Now it was Hindemith's turn. His case was more complicated.
Although he had set many a "frivolous" text to music, although
he had a Jewish wife and after 1933 continued to perform abroad
with Jewish colleagues, it was not easy to get at him: Paul Hindemith was the most productive and talented composer of the
younger generation of German composers, he had a great following among the young, he enjoyed an enormous international
prestige, and—he was "Aryan." When the agitation against him
began, Wilhelm Furtwängler, the great conductor of the Berlin
Philharmonic Orchestra and one-time composition student of
Max von Schillings, took up Hindemith's defense in a lengthy
article in the *Deutsche Allgemeine Zeitung* (November 25, 1934).
He described Hindemith as a man "who was also racially purely
Germanic, a decided 'German' type, German in his simple
craftsmanlike solidity and in his straight, robust character, as in the
chastity and reserve of his relatively rare emotional outbursts. . . .
His last work, the Symphony from the opera 'Mathis der Maler,'
has corroborated this impression anew." Unquestionably, with

this opera, for which he had chosen the life of the sixteenth-century German painter Matthias Grünewald, writing the libretto himself "in seven pictures," Hindemith had tried to create a work of a distinctly German character, in subject matter, in feeling, and in the endeavor to relate the opera to German music of the past. It was an attempt at an honest compromise in which he was neither selling his art nor his soul. Indeed, in the third "picture" he rises to a defense of freedom of thought; showing the preparations on the marketplace of Mainz for the burning of heretical books, he introduces the protagonist, Dean of the Cathedral of Mainz:

"Rome cannot tolerate resistance. The books must burn." Cardinal Albrecht von Brandenburg, Bishop of Mainz, rejoins:

"Against the spirit I will not offend."

And the Dean answers:

"There is one spirit only, that of obedience. A priest who resists must fall."

To believe that the Gestapo did not read the libretto before performance of the opera was forbidden underestimates the methodic thoroughness of their work. This passage was an open critique of the book burnings that had accompanied the take-over of the Nazis. Hindemith had dared to challenge the regime by making it clear that thought control and burning of books was too high a price to pay for acceptance by the regime. The Nazis, on the other hand, had to ponder what might happen if the scene sketched above were recited on the open stage. Might it not provoke public demonstrations in the Berlin Opera house?[2] The opera was forbidden; Furtwängler had to content himself with the performance of the symphony based on "Mathis der Maler." Furtwängler's attempt to save Hindemith for Germany was in vain:

2. Such demonstrations did indeed take place. On the evening of November 25, 1934, the day on which Furtwängler had published his defense of Hindemith, he conducted *Tristan* before a full house. Although Göring and Goebbels sat in their loges, an ovation greeted Furtwängler before he lifted the baton; an ovation that did not seem to end concluded the evening. That same night Göring is reported to have declared to Hitler that Furtwängler was endangering the regime's authority: the public had in fact demonstrated against the regime (Geissmar, 130).

"In a world so unspeakably poor in true creative musical talent," said he, in the concluding words of his appeal, "we cannot afford to lose a man like Hindemith." The Reichsminister thought otherwise. At a mass meeting in the Berlin Sportpalast on December 7, 1934, Goebbels rejected Furtwängler's defense of Hindemith: "We protest in the most energetic terms to have that type of artist characterized as German; we record the fact of his purely Germanic blood merely as the most drastic proof for how strongly the Jewish-intellectualistic infection has taken hold of our national body." That same month Furtwängler resigned all of his offices and positions in protest. But not for long. In a personal meeting with Goebbels in February, 1935, he capitulated. In a public statement he expressed regret that his article should have been interpreted in a political light: "It had never been my intention to interfere with the direction of the government's artistic policies which, also in my opinion, as a matter of course must be determined by the Führer and the minister in charge" (Wulf, 373–78).

Furtwängler was unquestionably the greatest conductor that Germany had at the time; his intention was noble, his initiative took courage. Still, it must be understood: Furtwängler's capitulation was the logical outcome of his accepting the premises of the national socialistic *Kulturpolitik*: complete subordination of art to race and politics. The lesson was inescapable: one cannot fight the works of totalitarianism if one embraces its ideology, even if only for tactical reasons. Furtwängler remained, muzzled and safe. Hindemith left.

Stefan Zweig, following these events with increasing alarm, asked Strauss to delay the performance of *Die schweigsame Frau* "in order to avoid any connection with the events in the musical world (Furtwängler, and so on)" (February 18, 1935). Strauss replied that now that Hitler and Goebbels had given their official consent to the performance there was no way to delay it. "Fate must take its course." That he too worried about the future appears from the end of his letter: "Should I have the good fortune to receive one or several new libretti from you, let us agree that nobody will ever know about it nor about my setting them to music. Once the score is finished, it will go into a safe that will be opened only when we both consider the time propitious" (February 20, 1935). And in a later letter he writes: "We will keep the matter confidential until we both deem the time right to come out with it" (February 26, 1935). Zweig reminded Strauss of his obligation as one of those great composers whose letters and whose decisions, like those of Brahms and Wagner, will one day become universal cultural property. "A Richard Strauss is privileged to take in public what is his right; he must not seek refuge in secrecy. No one should ever be able to say that you have shirked your responsibility" (February 23, 1935). These words were written two months after Furtwängler's resignation and only days before his capitulation. Zweig was impressed and encouraged by Furtwängler's stand. Surely, Strauss, whose achievement and position in Germany exceeded that of Furtwängler's, could do no less.

Yet, there was in his repeated refusal to continue his collaboration with Strauss in secret also the determination to observe his own responsibilities as a writer of world-wide renown, as friend and biographer of Romain Rolland, the ardent pacifist, as a man who had constantly worked for peace and international understanding.

If in the beginning Zweig was courting Strauss, now Strauss, deadly afraid that the one man who could write to suit his taste and talent might escape his grasp, courts Zweig with ever growing desperation. While he is nearing the end of *Die schweigsame Frau* he casts about for new opera subjects. He proposes a literary theme; Zweig rejects it. Zweig proposes new themes, Strauss rejects some of them, wants to see more of others. In the four years of their collaboration, eighteen different topics had been discussed, thirteen during the last year and a half. Two-thirds of the proposals came from Zweig (Abert, 11–12). One of them for illustration: In an episode from the end of the Thirty Years' War, a Swedish commander has laid siege to a German fortress, vowing he will accept only surrender. The situation within the fortress is desperate; the supply of food and ammunition is running dangerously low. The German commander swears he will never surrender; his men (and his wife) stay with him. The Swedes, determined to take the fortress by storm, give the Germans half an hour to surrender. Tension rises. But instead of the artillery barrage expected, bells begin to ring, messengers come running. A parliamentarian with a white flag approaches. Peace has been signed. The hostile commanders meet. Aware that only minutes earlier they had been bent on mutual destruction, they measure each other grimly, gradually relax, and finally embrace amid general jubilation. Zweig can develop his ideas of peace and heroism as not confined to war (August 21, 1934). Strauss responds with enthusiasm. In a follow-up letter he proposes to add a love affair between the commander's wife and his lieutenant (September 21, 1934). Zweig is dismayed. Obviously, he finds it "kitschig," but tones that down to "operatic in the unfortunate sense of the word" (October 3, 1934). And now Strauss, in a moment of deeply moving truth and self-insight, thunders: "Don't you understand that I need something that will inspire the flow of melodies that can touch the heart? Your ideas of heroism and world peace won't do it—a love affair will" (October 10, 1934). (The episode, which in 1938 became the opera *Der Friedenstag*, bears the name of Zweig's friend Joseph Gregor as librettist, hiding by necessity Zweig's part in its conception.) Already earlier, Strauss had confessed with supreme candor: "Must one become seventy years old to recognize that one's greatest strength lies in creating kitsch?" (January 21, 1934).

Zweig, more and more conscious of the increasingly untenable collaboration between a Jewish writer and the President of the Reichsmusikkammer under the Nazis, torments himself with the problem of how to dissolve the bonds between Strauss and himself without offending the master and—more importantly—without hurting the composer's rejuvenated Muse. Zweig must find another librettist for Strauss. He proposes one poet after another. He praises Lernet-Holenia to the skies. Strauss's reaction: "Herr Lernet-Holenia has had his two so-called comedies, *Alkestis* and

Potiphar's Wife, sent to me, and after reading them with indignation, I frankly don't know what to think of you. You cannot seriously believe that a man capable of publishing such silly, tasteless, and witless stuff could write a libretto for me?" Aware of Zweig's Achilles heel, he concludes: "No, dear Herr Zweig, this will not do. If you desert me now, now that you have written your admirable libretto, *Die schweigsame Frau*, I have no choice left but to retire" (April 22, 1935).

Zweig tries again, this time with a good friend of his, Joseph Gregor, author of a *History of the World Theater*. Gregor, in seventh heaven over the prospect of collaborating with Richard Strauss, sends him a sketch of a Semiramis libretto—a topic that had long tempted the composer. Strauss writes to Zweig: "You must have read Gregor's fetus by now. Any critique is superfluous. A philologist's childish fairytale. . . . Once and for all, please stop urging new poets upon me!" (May 17, 1935). Zweig tries to talk sense to the composer. Surely, Strauss must see which way the wind is blowing. "What a pity that I cannot work for you freely and openly. But the official measures instead of becoming milder and more conciliatory have only grown harsher. You will discover yourself, I fear, that the cultural development will more and more go to the side of the extremists" (May 19, 1935). But Strauss is beyond reasoning. He rejects one proposal after another in the hope of luring Zweig back to the collaboration that has produced such splendid fruit. Zweig promises the closest cooperation with Gregor. Strauss writes: "Your cooperation with Gregor makes my skin crawl. Why do you insist *à tout prix* on saddling me with an erudite philologist? My librettist is Zweig; he needs no collaborators" (June 13, 1935). And later, with increasing impatience: "I don't compose camouflaged operas. Texts invented by Zweig I will compose only under the name of Zweig" (June 28, 1935).

Strauss stuck to Zweig to the bitter end. The première of *Die schweigsame Frau* was to take place in Dresden on June 24, 1935. Two days earlier, in the middle of a game of skat, Strauss demanded to see the program. When all dilatory tactics proved

fruitless, the program was finally produced: Zweig's name was not
on it. Strauss's face flushed in hot anger: "You can do as you damn
please," he erupted. "I am leaving tomorrow morning." No one
who knew Strauss doubted for a minute that he meant what
he said, even though Hitler and Goebbels were expected to attend
(as it happened, they were absent). The result was confusion
worse confounded. In the end, the name of Stefan Zweig was
placed on the program. The man responsible for the decision to do
so was dismissed from his post at the Dresden Opera soon
thereafter.

Unquestionably loyal as Strauss was, in political matters he
demanded complete subordination. In the summer of 1934 Zweig
was in England. Strauss writes: "You were shadowed in London
and your magnificent conduct has been found 'correct and politically beyond reproach' " (August 2, 1934). As eager as he was to
please Strauss, Zweig must have squirmed from embarrassment
upon receiving an official record card of "good conduct" from the
hated regime. How self-evident it appeared to Strauss that Zweig
had to make all concessions required appears from the tone of
the instructions, not to say orders, that he issued: "Dear Herr
Zweig. In the interest of our *Schweigsame Frau* I should like to
request that you withdraw from the International Music Club, or
at any rate I recommend that you have your name withdrawn from
the list of advisers" (February 5, 1935). Zweig was surprised. He
declined to follow suit, but not because Strauss had gone too far—
under no circumstances did he wish to let it come to a break—
but because he "did not know whether the club still functioned,"
because "the club was apolitical," because it had on its program
six operas, three of German origin, one, *Arabella*, by Richard
Strauss, etc. In the end, the author of *Erasmus* (1934) rose to the
occasion: "For me to withdraw my name would be a demonstration on my part that would make out an enterprise to be political
which never was. A *sacrificio d'intelletto* always causes nothing
but harm" (February 18, 1935). Of his beloved Erasmus he had
said: "He resolutely resisted any attempt to force him to take a

religious or political stand. Independent thinking was a matter of course for him" (*Erasmus*, 11).

The closer the première comes, the more nervous Strauss grows. From Dresden, where he attends the rehearsals, he writes: "Here the rumor is making the rounds that you have assigned your royalties to the Jewish Emergency Fund. I have denied it" (June 13, 1935). It was in fact true. Zweig did not respond; nor did he change his decision.

But the finale is already shaping up. *Die schweigsame Frau* will be performed at the famous Dresden Opera in June, 1935. The rehearsals exceed Strauss's most sanguine expectations. He is full of joy and anticipation and keeps up a furious correspondence with Zweig, always thinking ahead of his coming works. But Zweig by now has made up his mind that the political situation has ruled out further collaboration with his beloved master. He has long enough searched for a way to take the sting out of his refusal. The time has come to speak plainly.

On June 15, 1935, Zweig pens a letter to Strauss in which he states the reasons why collaboration between them is no longer possible. For the first time he mentions things he has carefully avoided so far. He speaks of the inevitable sense of solidarity that he feels with his Jewish fellow artists and fellow men persecuted by the Nazis. The work on *Die schweigsame Frau* puts him into the position of seeming collaboration with an official representative of the Third Reich. After all, this is what Strauss as President of the Reichsmusikkammer is. And now he alludes to two events that he never mentioned before, although they go back to the very beginning of the new regime and they stirred angry criticism of Richard Strauss abroad. Early in 1933 Bruno Walter was scheduled to lead the Berlin Philharmonic Orchestra. Inquiring at the Ministry what the official position was, in view of threats made against him, he was advised that should he conduct, "everything in the hall will be smashed to pieces" (Marek, 273). Walter left town—Richard Strauss conducted. Similarly, in June 1933, when Toscanini cancelled his engagement to conduct *Parsifal* and *Die Meistersinger von Nürnberg* at Bayreuth, Richard Strauss took

over. Again, he was panned in the foreign press. Stefan Zweig
mentioned two events about which Strauss was extremely sensitive.

The letter reached the composer in Dresden, where he was
attending rehearsals for *Die schweigsame Frau*. Strauss was furious:

> Your letter of the 15th is driving me to distraction! This Jewish obstinacy!
> Enough to make an anti-Semite of a man! This pride of race, this
> feeling of solidarity! Do you believe that I am ever, in any of my
> actions, guided by the thought that I am a "German" (perhaps, *qui le sait*)?
> Do you believe that Mozart composed as an "Aryan"? I know only
> two types of people: those with and those without talent. The people
> [*das Volk*] exist for me only at the moment they become audience.
> Whether they are Chinese, Bavarians, New Zealanders, or Berliners
> leaves me cold. What matters is that they pay the full price for admission.
> . . . Who told you that I have exposed myself politically? Because I
> have conducted a concert in place of Bruno Walter? That I did for
> the orchestra's sake. Because I substituted for Toscanini? That I did for
> the sake of Bayreuth. . . . Because I ape the President of the Reich
> Music Chamber? That I do only for good purposes and to prevent
> greater disasters! I would have accepted this troublesome honorary
> office under any government. But neither Kaiser Wilhelm nor Herr
> Rathenau [the Jewish Minister of Foreign Affairs of the Weimar
> Republic] offered it to me. . . ."

The letter never reached Zweig. It was intercepted by the
Gestapo and sent by the "Reichsstatthalter in Sachsen" in person
to Hitler. Now things happen fast. A representative of Goebbels
visits Strauss, shows him the letter, and asks him to resign as
President of the Reichsmusikkammer "for reasons of health."
Strauss, finally awakening to the brutal reality of living and working under a dictatorship, is beside himself. The indignity of having
been placed under surveillance, of having a private letter sent
abroad opened—Zweig was in Switzerland—is more than he can
bear. He might have insisted on speaking with Goebbels first.
Instead, he resigns on the spot.

The fearless Strauss, who had been playing with dragons, now
gets a case of the jitters. He turns to Hitler himself, hoping to be
exonerated; he had written, after all, a private letter, and in a fit
of anger. He asks "most humbly" for an audience. He will explain

everything in person (Marek, 282–83). Strauss never received an answer. From now on the Nazis eye him with cold suspicion, making use of him, however, as the occasion demands. Upon request, he composed the hymn for the Olympic Games in Germany in 1936. He wrote a *Japanische Festmusik* in honor of the Japanese royal family in 1940. He tells his friends that these are the payments that he has to make to the national socialistic account for the debts he owes—and they are considerable: his former librettist was "non-Aryan"; his present librettist is Jewish; so is his daughter-in-law; he has to protect his two grandchildren on whom he dotes and whom he keeps in his villa at Garmisch; his publisher, Adolph Fürstner, is Jewish (so in fact is his copyist, who emigrated to Paris and to whom he sends the score of *Die schweigsame Frau* for the fair copy). The Nazis, aware of his prestige value, keep their part of the bargain. He and his family are never molested.

It might be mentioned that Zweig's letter of June 15 that gave rise to all this is lost. Its contents can be reconstructed from Strauss's answer. Strauss, who was known to have a terrible temper, may have destroyed it in anger. Another lost letter of Stefan Zweig to Richard Strauss has been discovered and published (Arens, 122–24). It is of special interest, because it was written shortly afterwards, on June 29, 1935. With perfect courtesy, Zweig comes back to the issue between them: Since he can no longer collaborate with Strauss, he offers to work with Gregor, and go over his libretto with him, page for page, so that Strauss will be pleased with the book he will receive. In this way "all bitterness and troubles will end. I don't wish to see you attacked again because of your collaboration with me; nor do I want the relationship that binds me to you misinterpreted as self-seeking ambition as if I wished to enjoy a status of special tolerance in Germany."

Tatiana had written her second letter to Onegin. Now the Prince was courting her and she refused. Strauss understood. Nothing he could now say would ever rekindle the flame of their former friendship and collaboration. He felt the need to justify himself in the eyes of posterity. Early in July, 1935, he wrote a memorandum and penned some related notes on the events (see pp. 107–110 below). Writing four days after his resignation as President of the Reichsmusikkammer, Strauss is now forced to recognize what price an artist making common cause with dictatorship has to pay:

> It is a sad time when an artist of my rank has to ask a brat of a minister [Goebbels] what he may set to music and what he may have performed. I, too, belong to the nation of "servants and waiters." * I almost envy my friend Stefan Zweig, persecuted for his race, who now definitely refuses to work with me in public or in secret. . . . I regret that the "artist" Zweig cannot rise above "political fashions."

While Strauss, moving in obvious contradictions, speaks of the events in Germany as "political fashions," Stefan Zweig, great historian that he was, could not deceive himself about the seriousness of the world situation. He saw the thunderclouds mass over Germany and he knew that the storm now in the making would soon sweep over the whole world. Not "political fashions"— mankind was the issue. He felt it deeply. The outbreak of the war found him first in the United States, and then in Brazil, admired and honored, but incapable of bearing the horrors and destruction of the war even from a safe distance. Having followed the victorious march of the Axis powers for three years, he and his second wife put an end to their lives. "I greet all my friends! May they live to see the dawn after the long night is over! I, all too impatient, am going on alone" (February 22, 1942; Allday, 238).

Richard Strauss, in the meantime, anxious to go on composing, turned to Gregor. He mistreated the poor professor terribly. One has to read the Strauss-Gregor correspondence to believe it. The good Gregor complains, but goes on suffering. His adoration of Strauss was such that he even consented to have the correspondence published. Zweig, referred to in their correspondence as "our friend," had kept his word, counseling Gregor, criticizing and revising *Der Friedenstag*. Later Gregor furnishes the libretti for *Daphne* and *Die Liebe der Danae*. Of one reproach expressed by an outstanding American opera critic that "Strauss was misled

* See footnote, p. 109.

by the poor libretto [*Daphne*]" (Lang, 263) the composer may be
absolved: the present correspondence as well as that between
Strauss and Gregor are witness that he turned to Gregor only in
desperation.

One last word on Zweig's judgment on Richard Strauss, the
composer. From the correspondence emerges nothing but undiluted
admiration. But Zweig was much too fine a musical connoisseur
not to be aware of Strauss's weaknesses, and Strauss made it easy
for him to recognize them: he was an unusually honest and
objective critic of his own work. Zweig reports on a closed rehearsal
of *Die aegyptische Helena* that they attended together in the
Festspielhaus of Salzburg. It was perfectly dark in the room.
Suddenly Strauss began to drum on the back of the chair with his
fingers, softly and impatiently: "Bad," he whispered, "very bad.
Devoid of any musical idea." After a few minutes, again: "If only
I could strike that out. Oh God, oh God, how empty this is and
too long, much too long." A bit later: "Now look here, this is
good!" (*Welt*, 336). At a personal meeting, during which they
discussed the libretto of *Die schweigsame Frau*, Strauss instructed
Zweig on his deficiencies as a composer which he, the librettist,
had to keep in mind. As a seventy-year-old musician he did not
possess the musical inspiration he had as a younger man.
Symphonic works would now be out of his reach. But a libretto,
words, a plot, acting, they still inspired him to musical dramatiza-
tion. "Long melodies, such as Mozart invented, don't come to me.
I find only short themes. But I do know how to turn such a theme,
how to paraphrase it, and to get out of it all that is in it." "I was
astonished about such frankness," adds Zweig, "for really it is
rare to find in Strauss a melody going beyond a few measures; but
how these few measures, say, of the waltz in the *Rosenkavalier*, are
then developed into a rich and perfect fullness!" (*Welt*, 336).

On one issue Zweig and Strauss had a serious difference of
opinion. From the very beginning, Zweig had felt that comedy and
comic opera should not be the exclusive property of great opera
houses and the wealthy public. In a letter now lost, he proposed

to Strauss to make cuts in *Die schweigsame Frau* and to make an arrangement for smaller—and less elitist—musical forces. Strauss responded in characteristically uninhibited form: "What odd ideas you have! Why should I become 'popular' at any price, that is, tied to the rabble and performed in every low-class theater?" (June 28, 1935). To adapt great and difficult works of art to the needs of the little opera pubs, Strauss goes on, he might as well leave to Lehár and Puccini. He himself, on the contrary, is doing everything in his power to persuade Goebbels to create the cultural centers and the musical forces needed to perform the great masterworks of the German opera literature as the composers wrote them. "For this reason, an adaptation for normal theaters, as you propose, is out of the question. . . . I have never had the talent to write what can be performed easily; that is the special gift of inferior musicians."

In the letter believed lost (June 29, 1935) alluded to earlier, Zweig responds to Strauss's harangue in his usual calm tone: "If the composer himself, with all his authority, proposes cuts rather than the director accidentally present, this I cannot consider a concession. . . . As long as we do not have the ideal Festspielhaus theater, which will always attract an elite of artists and listeners, shortening and lightening seem to me a boon to the work of art" (Arens, 123).

Zweig's intuition was proved right by the events. When, after the end of the war, *Die schweigsame Frau* finally entered the German and Austrian opera stages, it was in fact considerably reduced in length, and Strauss himself recommended cuts (Krause, 346–47).

Zweig's feelings about *Die schweigsame Frau* are sober in the extreme. We know of them through a letter to his wife, written two days after the première (June 26, 1935):

By now I have gotten a general idea of what happened in Dresden. People agree on only one point, that the city was in the grip of an African heat wave. . . . As for the opera itself, one thing is certain, it is *very* much too long, secondly, it is an atrociously difficult work and so the very opposite of my original conception of it—not a light opera, but overloaded with all the *raffinements* and really oppressive because it is too replete. Single passages are said to be outstanding and the first act well rounded. Then it gets to be tiring, like *Arabella* and *The Egyptian Helena*. His technique remains intact. But the dynamic isn't there. . . . This appears to be the most difficult of Strauss's difficult operas. I am anxious to hear it on the radio. Perhaps he will, by then, have made the necessary cuts" (Alsberg, 267–68).

Obviously, much of his judgment is a reflection of the reviews and certainly also of reports from friends—but not all. We know from Zweig himself that Strauss, in his villa in Garmisch, "sitting at the piano, with his long, slender fingers, played, little by little, the whole opera for me from the sketch book" (*Welt*, 338). Zweig's musical ear and perception were undoubtedly capable of forming an idea of the whole. Also, Zweig received from Strauss, upon his request and per agreement, the piano score of *Die schweigsame Frau* (Zweig to Strauss: March 14, 1935; April 26, 1935; Strauss to Zweig: April 29, 1935). Zweig's judgment, in essence, was not far removed from the perceptive summary of Paul Henry Lang who, fully aware of the part played by the commonplace in Strauss's work—"his apparent commonplace can conceal qualities that are not commonplace at all"—has this to say about the opera:

The Silent Woman is bright, hypersophisticated, and inordinately clever. All of its first act is masterly in plan and execution, and though later the opera often sags, there are many other felicitous scenes. The secret of the success of this opera is, of course, that there are no pretensions; everything, or almost everything, is on the surface, and no attempt is made at profundities. But this surface is quite pleasing, for Strauss lavishes care and imaginative reality upon the details with which he surrounds his characters, and the sensitive treatment of the principal figures—the old man who hates noise and the young woman who takes pity on him—discloses unexpected qualities in this old master, who for years had been merely coasting along on his phenomenal skill and savoir-faire.

The thrice-told tale of Don Pasquale—of the amorous old guardian outwitted by a clever young couple—is repeated with skill, cunning, and a touch of almost disarming irony by a composer whose knowledge of the lyric was consummate. Being a true buffa, *The Silent Woman* has many ensembles, and they are devilishly difficult—so difficult, in fact, that only the most extraordinary virtuosity can do justice to them. The composer used several thousand board feet of musical lumber to panel the ensembles, which at times become breathless; a top-notch company, however, can carry them off" (Lang, 261–62).

The most important part of Zweig's critique of *Die schweigsame Frau* are the words: "an atrociously difficult work and so *the very opposite of my original conception of it*" (italics by this writer). What had been his original conception? At the beginning of their collaboration on the opera Strauss asked Zweig's counsel concerning the ever-present question in operatic music: should he use secco recitative or spoken dialogue? He feared that sung recitative with its "Mozartian" simplicity did not fit his style. Zweig, in one of his most interesting letters (December 19, 1932), fully approves the idea of spoken dialogue as fitting the style of musical comedy, but suggests that it go with a light orchestral accompaniment: few instruments, few measures of thematic figuration, instruments of a "sharp" sort such as flute, saxophone, drum, piccolo, violin. He is thinking of a kind of modern "scansion." The instrumental accompaniment might assume an ironic tone, when it, for example, parodies the emotional speech of the barber. In such prose passages music should only stimulate, sparkling like champagne, not satisfy, so that one enjoys it doubly once it begins to flow again.

In Zweig's idea of musical comedy the important element is not so much how to use spoken dialogue, but how to adapt music to the spirit of lightness that animates not only the dialogue, but the whole atmosphere and action in comedy. This lightness Zweig missed in *Die schweigsame Frau*. Strauss did not forget Zweig's ideas about musical comedy. It seems as if it had taken some time for him to absorb them. He finally applied them in his last opera, *Capriccio*, which goes back to an idea initiated by Zweig and discussed with Strauss in their correspondence, but finally worked out—after disastrous failure with Gregor—in collaboration with Clemens Krauss, the Viennese opera conductor, who functioned then as general intendant of the Munich Opera. An eminent historian of opera says of *Capriccio*:

The score is of a stylized rococo quality and is held throughout in the mood of chamber music. A full orchestra is required but is used for the most part only in small combinations; the sonority of the string sextet, first heard in the introduction, runs like a thread through the opera. The words are made to come clearly through the polyphonic orchestral texture, being conveyed in lifelike dialogue and broadly designed ensembles (Grout, 520).

Strauss himself held *Capriccio* in high esteem; when asked whether he wanted to compose another opera, he replied: "It's only possible to leave *one* will" (Krause, 434).

Perhaps Strauss intended, in his "last will," to execute the wish and vision of Stefan Zweig, the beloved librettist of his old age, collaboration with whom was shattered, after a blessed beginning, by the emergence of a regime that preached and practiced chauvinistic arrogance, hatred of all aspirations for international understanding, and contempt for human freedom and dignity. Art has never flourished under such regimes. This Stefan Zweig had always known; Richard Strauss had to learn it, reluctantly, in many painful lessons.

EDWARD E. LOWINSKY

Bibliography

Abert	Anna Amalie Abert, "Stefan Zweigs Bedeutung für das Alterswerk von Richard Strauss," in *Festschrift Friedrich Blume zum 70. Geburtstag*, ed. Anna Amalie Abert and Wilhelm Pfannkuch (Kassel, 1963), pp. 7–15.
Allday	Elizabeth Allday, *Stefan Zweig: A Critical Biography* (London, 1972).
Alsberg	*Stefan and Friderike Zweig: Their Correspondence 1912–1942*, translated and edited by Henry G. Alsberg with the assistance of Erna MacArthur (New York, 1954).
Arens	*Stefan Zweig im Zeugnis seiner Freunde*, ed. Hanns Arens (Munich and Vienna, 1968).
Erasmus	Stefan Zweig, *Triumph und Tragik des Erasmus von Rotterdam* (Vienna, 1935).
Geissmar	Berta Geissmar, *Musik im Schatten der Politik* (Zurich, 1945).
Grout	Donald Jay Grout, *A Short History of Opera* (2d ed., New York and London, 1965).

Krause   Ernst Krause, *Richard Strauss: The Man and his Work*
            (Boston, 1969).

Lang   Paul Henry Lang, *Critic at the Opera* (New York, 1971).

Marek   George R. Marek, *Richard Strauss: The Life of a Non-
            Hero* (New York, 1967).

Prater   D. A. Prater, *European of Yesterday: A Biography of
            Stefan Zweig* (Oxford, 1972).

Welt   Stefan Zweig, *Die Welt von Gestern: Erinnerungen eines
            Europäers* (Berlin, 1962).

Wulf   Joseph Wulf, *Musik im Dritten Reich: Eine Dokumentation*
            (Gütersloh, 1963).

The Letters of
Richard Strauss and Stefan Zweig

My dear Herr Doctor,

Professor Kippenberg[1] has kindly encouraged me to send you the enclosed privately printed Mozart letter;[2] it may not be suitable for the public but may be a small pleasure for connoisseurs. I am delighted at least to have an opportunity to express in a modest way my great affection and admiration for you.

I have been wondering whether I might visit you some time and present a musical project to you. But when I admire somebody I am ill at ease. If I knew that you would not consider the hour lost, I would gladly call on you. With best regards, respectfully,

Stefan Zweig

My dear Herr Zweig,

Your kind letter and the delightful Mozart gave me great pleasure. Thank you so much! You will be interested to know that I own an original letter of the Divine[3]—also addressed to his cousin; unfortunately, this letter is so inoffensive that it could be read openly even in a Mozart Club. I was particularly pleased to learn about your intention to visit me, and with a musical project at that. I will be here all winter. A modest guest room is always at your disposal. Please let me know by telephone (Garmisch

2178), to make sure that I am not in Munich when you want to visit. May I confess what I would like to get from the creator of *Das Lamm des Armen, Volpone,* and the magnificent *Fouché*? Among the types of women represented in my operas, I lack a type that I would love to set to music for the stage: the woman adventurer, the grande dame as a spy. I am old-fashioned enough to be fascinated by Augustin Scribe's *Ein Glass Wasser* [*Le Verre d'Eau*] and Victorien Sardou's *Letzter Brief* [*Les Pattes de Mouche*] and I do not agree with Hofmannsthal who thinks that an intelligent play of intrigue is no longer acceptable today.[4] It would depend on what it is and how it's done.

But let's discuss this when you come. With best wishes, respectfully,

Dr. Richard Strauss

Salzburg, Kapuzinerberg 5
November 3, 1931

My dear Herr Doctor,

My sincere thanks for your important letter. I will take the liberty of inquiring in the second half of November whether my visit would be convenient. I only would like to ask that you permit me to stay in a hotel. As a houseguest I am never sure whether I am disturbing.

I would like to discuss two projects, and they are very different. The first seems more significant and important to me, although it will, at first glance, seem the lesser to you; let me just briefly allude to it. I believe it will win you over by its enormous potential, when I have a chance to present it in detail. I am referring to a dancing pantomime in grand style—please do not reject the idea out of hand; it is not a choreographic play but a presentation of *the* universal and generally comprehensible problem of music, and of art altogether. In specific terms, I visualize a work, clear in its outlines, universally understandable, playable on every stage in the world, in all languages, before any audience high-brow and low-brow; at the same time challenging the man of music to highest accomplishment—a work that comprises all contrasts of the arts, from the tragic to the light-hearted, from the Apollonian to the Dionysian, timeless, a work in which a man and a musician like yourself can attain the epitome of his life's task. The plan, completed in detail, has been in my desk for ten years. I have never shown it to anyone and only thought of you, but did not approach you out of consideration for Hofmannsthal, as a matter of tact. I visualize a timeless dimension as for *Elektra*—a full, majestic presentation of grandeur and unfolding development. If I seem to praise my work, please do not misunderstand. All I want to say is that, by suggesting this project to you, it is not my intention to divert you to a *minor work* as you might be misled to assume when I use the term dancing pantomime. I believe, to the contrary, that you have reached a level of life and accomplishment that should not be wasted on minor works; a level at which you ought to reserve your inspiration for works that embrace the full scope of your capacity. And I fantasize that this work would have a dimension beyond that of any opera.

Of course, the material is such that I could also formulate it as an opera libretto. Yet I conceive of it as *still* more universal in its wordlessness. The pantomime is broken by a human voice only once, when it reaches its internal peak; and I visualize it fearsomely beautiful when the audience, wholly immersed in the language of musical instruments, suddenly is shaken by hearing that most holy and sublime of all instruments, the human larynx.

The second project is a merry, lively, fast-moving opera,[5] easy to write, easy to play, with classical figures: in the center a charming, witty, bubbling woman surrounded by a dozen persons, an entertaining milieu. I appreciate only those stories or novels that have enough visual impact to be suitable for movies, and only those operas that can be understood without reading a libretto beforehand or during the performance; an opera must be comprehensible as a stage presentation, otherwise it burdens the opus and splits the viewer's attention. I see works of art in a European, truly universal, dimension, not tied, because of their cumbersome apparatus, to a few large cities; it should be possible to perform these in small places, they should be able to nest anywhere like birds. This goal ought to be attainable without concessions to literary quality, provided the precondition is met, of a light, lean construction and a commonly understandable appeal. To be frank, I see the last Hofmannsthal libretti as too heavily burdened with the search for style and symbolism, both beyond the normal vision of an unsophisticated audience not equipped with special glasses for reading libretti. I am sure you will not misunderstand. I am well aware of the scope of Hofmannsthal's vision, a scope that only the élan of his language could fully embrace. But I am afraid this desire to reach what one might call a higher dimension was attainable only at the expense of its effective communication. The general comprehensibility of a work of art for one and all may not be the condition for its quality, but it is its last and decisive test.

I have inflicted these details on you as an indication that the pantomime is not a weird or odd suggestion: it could be performed as much in Innsbruck as in Milwaukee or Seville, and not only at the twelve or twenty large opera houses of the world. Even your [ballet] *Josefslegende* seems to me too much tied to costume, ostentation, and style, and not enough universally understandable in its plot. You can see, Herr Doctor, that in approaching you I am not pulling some random project from my pocket; I am setting my sights as high as my appreciation of your work and yourself. And that is high indeed: there is nothing higher at this time.

Until about the fifteenth or sixteenth I will be immobilized by my work.[6] In any case I would come only after making sure by wire that my visit would not be inconvenient. Respectfully,

Stefan Zweig

Garmisch
November 5, 1931

My dear Herr Zweig,

Thank you cordially for your interesting and welcome letter. I will be in Munich between November 14 and 17—may I expect you around the twentieth? The better Garmisch chalet-type hotels are all closed at the moment, the remaining "inns" are quite undesirable, so you must give my wife and me the pleasure of staying with us. We will not disturb you and you can do as you please. With best wishes, respectfully,

Dr. Richard Strauss

Salzburg, Kapuzinerberg 5
[First half of November, 1931]

My dear Herr Doctor,

My warmest thanks for your kind letter. I will be in Garmisch on the twenty-first around noon—from the seventeenth to the twentieth in the evening I shall be in Munich, Hotel Leinfelder. Please do not think of me as ungrateful or rude if I prefer to stay in a small inn in Garmisch, but I have an almost *heathen* bashfulness about staying in the home of a productive person: the feeling that I might disturb would be too oppressive. I *very* much look forward to seeing you; it will not matter if you do not have time for me on the twenty-first or twenty-second; I have plenty of work, and the time would not be wasted. Sincerely,

Stefan Zweig

I will phone on the twenty-first.

Garmisch
November 17, 1931

My dear Herr Zweig,

Just back from Munich, I find your kind letter. I announced my arrival for *Elektra* in Munich on Friday the twentieth, and will get there Friday 10:30 A.M. To save you the longer trip to Garmisch let me suggest that we meet in Munich. If you would kindly call me Friday at 11 A.M. in the Hotel Vierjahreszeiten, we could discuss the most pressing points at once and continue our conversation Saturday morning. Friday afternoon I will be occupied; in the evening I will have to attend to *Elektra*, and you are cordially invited.

I will await you without further confirmation on Friday 11 A.M. at the Vierjahreszeiten. Sincerely,

Dr. Richard Strauss

Garmisch
April 19, 1932

My dear Herr Zweig,

Have you been thinking about your delightful opera subject since we last met? I would very much like to do it and soon will have time to work on it. If you think that a personal conference would be worthwhile, I would be pleased to call on you in Salzburg after May 6 (from the first to the fifth I'll be in Berlin, and from then on will stay again in Garmisch); we could then chat in greater detail about your charming material and the possibilities for setting it to music. With good wishes, sincerely,

Dr. Richard Strauss

Salzburg, Kapuzinerberg 5
April 21, 1932

My dear Herr Doctor,

Thank you very much for your kind letter. I would have written long ago, but I knew of your triumphant trip in the South[7] and I spent most of my own winter working in Paris. Now I am off to Florence where I am to lecture on May 3—in Italian, may Dante forgive me—to be repeated in Milan on May 6. On May 8 I shall be back here or in Munich. Before I submit the project to you in final form, I would like to write an intermediate draft; perhaps I will be able to do this en route. I will adjust myself entirely to your schedule, whenever you have time and are in the mood. I do not mind at all coming to Munich, because I honor your time as the most precious in Germany. After May 8, then, I shall be free and happy to see you wherever I may. Respectfully,

Stefan Zweig

Garmisch
May 8, 1932

My dear Herr Zweig,

I am back from Berlin. Will you please let me know when your draft has reached the point that a personal meeting may be fruitful. Until June 10 I will be free any time; after that I plan to take a cure at Baden near Zurich for three weeks. With best wishes, respectfully,

Dr. Richard Strauss

Salzburg, Kapuzinerberg 5
[May, 1932]

Dear Herr Doctor,

Just back from Italy, I find your letter and am grateful. During these Pentecost holidays I shall try and see whether I can strike the right note to start and then will write you at once; after the tuning fork for one's verses is sounded, the rhythm rolls by itself. But to find the right style is a matter of inspiration. I shall try. And if I should fail, I'll be ready to turn over all the material and the draft to anybody whom you may choose, claiming nothing but the satisfaction of perhaps having given a small idea to a great man. I shall try to find a rhythm, then, and will report whether I have succeeded. Devotedly,

Stefan Zweig

Garmisch
May 27, 1932

My dear Herr Zweig,

From Tuesday, the thirty-first, to Thursday, second of June,
I shall be in Munich (Hotel Vierjahreszeiten). Could we meet
there? If it does not suit you or if it would interrupt your work too
much, I could equally well come to Salzburg on Wednesday noon,
arriving at twelve o'clock by car and returning to Munich in the
evening. Please drop me a note which arrangement is most
agreeable to you. With best wishes, respectfully,

Dr. Richard Strauss

Garmisch
June 13, 1932

My dear Herr Zweig,

Should you be unable to send me, during the next few days, the
promised draft of the contents of Sir Morosus* and if possible,
some finished scenes of the first act—I badly need them because my
composing time is during the summer—I want you to know that,
beginning June 18, I shall be in Baden near Zurich (Hotel
Verenahof). Gratefully remembering the beautiful noon hour in
your delightful home, I am with good wishes, also to your ladies,
sincerely,

Dr. Richard Strauss

* See note 5. Sir Morosus Blunt, bass, is one of the main parts in *Die
schweigsame Frau.*

Hotel Verenahof
Baden, Switzerland
June 24, 1932

My dear Herr Zweig,

Thank you very much for sending me the Morosus draft. Let
me repeat enthusiastically: it is enchanting—a born comic opera—

a comedy equal to the best of its kind—more suitable for music than even *Figaro* and the *Barber of Seville.*

Let me ask you urgently to complete the first act as soon as your other important tasks permit. I can't wait to work on it intensively. In the beginning it takes a while for me to get going and to find the right style. But as soon as half an act is drafted, the imagination runs by itself. With good wishes and thanks, also to Mrs. Zweig, sincerely,

Dr. Richard Strauss

Salzburg, Kapuzinerberg 5
June 26, 1932

My dear Herr Doctor,

I have a terribly bad conscience because I do not know whether I can work as promptly as I would like to; I am swamped with corrections and new drafts, and before the end of July I shall hardly be able to unload this Chimborazo of work.[8] I am *trying* to work in between and have made ample notes. My problem is to get the right élan, and that is difficult when one is so weighed down. But I will send you the first samples as soon as possible. For today, just my very best wishes for your cure, respectfully,

Stefan Zweig

Salizburg, Kapuzinerberg 5
July 27, 1932

Dear Herr Doctor,

The heavy load that weighs on me will soon be gone; a week from now my book *Marie Antoinette* will be finished and then I will be able to start on that text with all my enthusiasm. I trust that the relief will result in a little buoyancy, and I am looking forward to presenting to you the first sample here in Salzburg. I would have been most happy had I been able to devote myself fully to this work earlier, but one should never embark on something half-heartedly; only with full concentration. I am enormously looking forward to doing this task and am fully and most cordially at your disposal anywhere and anytime. Devotedly,

Stefan Zweig

Garmisch
July 28, 1932

Dear Herr Doctor,

Thank you for your kind letter. You can see that I respected your predicament, and did not badger you. Now I want to tell you that from August 15 I will be in Munich (Hotel Vierjahreszeiten) and will arrive in Salzburg on the twentieth.

It would be important to me to receive the first act of Morosus *before* I get to Salzburg (around August 10) so I can study it here at leisure; and then meet you in Salzburg with my considered agreement or, if necessary, with criticism that is not too improvised.

Will this be possible? I would be most grateful. In the meantime I am busy with the orchestration. I am, with keen anticipation and good wishes, respectfully,

Dr. Richard Strauss

P.S.   In Baden I read *Cagliostro* by A. Dumas. Did you know that it several times mentions Marie Antoinette's virginity?

Salzburg, Kapuzinerberg 5
August 12, 1932

My dear Herr Doctor,

Yesterday, at last, I mailed the last page of my new book and am free. I tried to write something, but cheerful and serious, sweet and bitter do not mix. In three days I will go to work seriously and hope to be able to show you something here in Salzburg. And then I shall be *wholly* at your disposal, and only what is *whole* is good. Devotedly,

Stefan Zweig

Salzburg, Kapuzinerberg 5
[Second half of August, 1932]

Dear Herr Doctor,

I have just returned to Salzburg, and want to let you know that, with the exception of this afternoon, I shall be at your disposal any time. So far I have drafted only the first two scenes, to find the right tone. If you approve of it I shall continue to work at once, and then I can come to Garmisch for 10 to 14 days to be at your disposal. The great burden of the book is off my shoulders, the turmoil of the festivals is almost over. As Goethe says, "der Ausblick frei," and now at last I also have the right inner peace of mind and good spirits. You won't be disappointed any longer by your devoted

Stefan Zweig

Salzburg, Kapuzinerberg 5
Friday, August 26, 1932

My dear Herr Doctor,

I shall leave Salzburg for two days, Saturday, Sunday, to be able to concentrate on the work without being disturbed. But I'll be back Monday. My wife and I would be pleased if Mrs. Strauss and you could join us for lunch or dinner either Monday or Tuesday—it could be in our house or downtown to save you the alpine effort of climbing Kapuzinerberg. Just let us know by telephone through the concierge of your hotel, my wife is here; any day and hour, and any place, are fine with us, we will accept your decision.

Your *Fidelio* was brilliant![9] We all were entranced. Devotedly,

Stefan Zweig

P.S.   Felix Bloch[10] tells me in a letter he will be happy to talk with you about the matter discussed.

Garmisch
August 29, 1932

[Postal card]
My dear Herr Zweig,

Because of the heat my wife and I went home yesterday, but I will be in Salzburg again Wednesday noon and hope to see you then. With good wishes, sincerely,

Dr. Richard Strauss

Garmisch
September 6, 1932

[Postal card]
My dear Herr Zweig,

Tomorrow we shall start on our trip to the Dolomites and expect to be in Pontresina (Hotel Saratz) on the ninth and tenth. It would be nice if you could send a few pages of the beginning to me there. From the eleventh I'll be here again and will stay all September. With best regards, also to Mrs. Zweig, your

Dr. Richard Strauss

[*Badgastein*
September 10, 1932
(postmark)]

[Picture postcard]
My dear Herr Doctor,

I came here for two days to work quietly. On Monday I'll be in Salzburg, and there I shall have a clear copy made of the entire beginning section. I think it's coming along fine. Devotedly,

Stefan Zweig

Salzburg, Kapuzinerberg 5
[About September 12, 1932]

Dear Herr Doctor,

   Here is the scene up to the point where the nephew of Morosus barges in, whereupon Sir Morosus at once gives up all his marriage plans and announces the nephew to be his heir, followed by the lively scenes with the actors. Simultaneously I have worked on the grand finale (sextet or octet), which is the end of the first act. Everything is going presto now, and you will soon hear again from your devoted

Stefan Zweig

P.S.   I finished the corrections on my book; *finally* I have my hands and mind free after this tome. Best regards to Mrs. Strauss.

Garmisch
September 14, 1932

My dear Zweig,

   Just back from Pontresina I find your welcome package. I can only repeat what I said after the preliminary reading: absolutely exquisite!

   Please continue without any hesitation. I would not know what to change. Possibly I may omit some repetitions, duplications, emphases. I won't be able to decide about this until I start composing, but this must not hamper you in any way from continuing in the style in which you have started.

   Thank you, and best wishes (also from my wife to you and Mrs. Zweig), sincerely,

Dr. Richard Strauss

Salzburg, Kapuzinerberg 5
September 17, 1932

Dear Herr Doctor,

I am not sending you the continuation, and the reason is not laziness but the opposite. I have decided to start my work with the great finale of the first act, and I am having fun weaving together the eight voices into a truly lively and rhythmic octet. You will like it. Once this main piece, which musically has great potential, is completed, the rest of the first act is easy. I am working on it continuously now, here and there, as ideas come to me. At the end of the month you will then have the complete first act, whose crowning will be the great, vivacious finale, and I am looking forward to it myself. Be assured of my commitment, for now I have the right momentum; it is a good omen to enjoy one's work so much.

With best regards to Mrs. Strauss, and good wishes, your devoted

Stefan Zweig

Gardone, Pensione Garda
[*October 5, 1932 (postmark)*]

[Picture postcard]
My dear Herr Doctor,

I am here finishing the first act in a most happy mood. I shall send it soon, perhaps I'll deliver it in person on my return. Devotedly,

Stefan Zweig

Garmisch
October 7, 1932

Dear Herr Zweig,

I received your welcome card and want to tell you that Herr Bloch has not yet called on me.

The *Arabella* orchestra score will be completed in a few days.

I have decided to have it published and have the "world premiere" (disgusting word) in Dresden next summer as soon as the score is available. If Herr Bloch seriously intends to compete with [Berlin music publisher Adolf] Fürstner, who is much interested in *Arabella* despite the hard times, we would have to come to an understanding soon—it is just because of those hard times that I would be obliged to give *Arabella* to the economically stronger publisher, much as I hate to be disloyal to good old Fürstner. Please let me know Herr Bloch's exact address right away, and also inform him that my son will be in Munich (Hotel Bristol) October 10 to 18 and will be able to conduct preliminary negotiations with him, unless Bloch prefers to come here in the next few days. I myself will be in Budapest from October 19 to 31, in Garmisch from November 2 to 5, and Hanover from November 12 to 14.

Good luck for the finale of act one, and best wishes, sincerely,

Dr. Richard Strauss

P.S.　Perhaps in passing through Salzburg on my way to Budapest I could see you for a moment at the railroad station: October 19; I'll let you know which train.

Gardone
October 8, 1932

Dear Herr Doctor,

Thank you so much for your kind letter. I am working quite hard here, and I expect to be able to finish the first act on Monday or Tuesday and then to mail it to you from Salzburg. On the way back I may take the Mittenwald train from Innsbruck, although it looks as if all suitable trains are already discontinued for the winter.

I shall write to Felix Bloch today. You have not heard from him probably because of the uncertainty and rush that dominate all things connected with the theater. I am sure he will be pleased to meet with your son in Berlin.

I might inquire, by wire or phone, if there should be an opportunity to drop by from Innsbruck, otherwise I shall mail the text from Salzburg, where I'll be on the fourteenth or fifteenth; the text, of course, is tentative. With kind regards to Mrs. Strauss, most devotedly,

Stefan Zweig

Garmisch
October 10, 1932

Dear Herr Zweig,

I would be delighted if you were to bring me the first act in person. Please wire me when you can be in Innsbruck. I'll then pick you up from the station by car. With best wishes,

Dr. Richard Strauss

[*Gardone*
October 11, 1932 (postmark)]

[Picture postcard]
Dear Herr Doctor,

I finished the first act today. It will be copied into a clean draft on the thirteenth and fourteenth, and will be in your hands on the fifteenth. I would then be delighted to see you when you pass through Salzburg. Devotedly,

Stefan Zweig

Garmisch
October 13, 1932

My dear Herr Zweig,

Warmest congratulations on the completion of the first act. I am eager to see it.

Because of the mild fall weather I have decided to go to Budapest by car. I shall arrive in Salzburg on *Tuesday, the eighteenth* after 5 P.M. and spend the night at the Hotel Oester-reichischer Hof. I'll phone you as soon as I get there.

In your letter before last, which discusses my son's visit with Herr Bloch in Berlin, I read between the lines that Bloch, after his initial readiness (following your first telephone conversation), is no longer as enthusiastic to purchase my opera *Arabella* as would have to be the condition if negotiations are to be successful.

My loyal publisher Fürstner is willing to forego *Arabella* only if another publisher is able to pay substantially higher royalties than he can afford; I therefore will have to think carefully whether to take this first step of disloyalty toward him; giving up *Arabella* would be a keen disappointment and a real loss of prestige for him.

Since your first friendly advice to approach Bloch burdens you with some small responsibility, I should like to ask you kindly to inquire once again from Bloch whether he is seriously interested in *Arabella*. You know my terms, and the production of the work (printing of score and piano score) costs additionally about 50,000 marks.

My son, Dr. Franz Strauss, will be in Berlin, Hotel Bristol, from Sunday on. Please write to him directly whether a visit with Herr Bloch is worth the trouble; I do not wish to be put in the position of having to *offer* Arabella to Herr Bloch unless he is firmly determined to purchase the work. Since you were so kind as to take the initiative in this matter, you must forgive me for asking you for your further good offices as intermediary, and to inform him in writing about the procedure as it follows from your correspondence with him. Best wishes, sincerely,

Dr. Richard Strauss

Salzburg, Kapuzinerberg 5
October 13, 1932

My dear Herr Doctor,

Herewith the remainder of the first act, to complete what you already have. I hope you like it and that the various parts are well balanced. Although Aminta, the main female part, does not stand out much in the first act, she dominates the second and third acts, whereas the barber, who has the main part here, is somewhat in the background later. Of course I am quite willing to make changes; up to now the work has not been labor but pleasure. Respectful regards,

Stefan Zweig

P.S.   I just received a letter from the head of the Felix Bloch company stating that he will attend the Hauptmann premiere in Vienna, but then immediately visit with your son in Berlin. Best regards to Mrs. Strauss.

[October 14, 1932
(postmark)]

[Picture postcard]
My dear Herr Zweig,
   The first act has just arrived, as promised. *"Bravi, bravi,* absolutely excellent," it says in *Cosi fan tutte.* I'll be in Salzburg, Tuesday 5 P.M.
   With whole-hearted congratulations and best wishes, also from my wife to you and Mrs. Zweig, most devotedly your

Dr. Richard Strauss

Salzburg, Kapuzinerberg 5
October 15, 1932

Dear Herr Doctor,
   I am delighted that you approve of the text. I am certain that the second act, which is still more lively, will not lag behind the first; also that it has been possible to draw all roles appealingly, which seems essential to me for a comedy. I am most happy that I will be able to talk with you in person in Salzburg on Tuesday.
   I know that the Felix Bloch company would be *happy,* in

principle, to purchase a work from you, but in general the theater people in Berlin are nowadays in a constant state of uncertainty; the chaos there is without parallel and explains, I suppose, why Herr Wreede has not called on you yet (he has just been to Vienna and Italy). But he will, of course, call on your son in Berlin at once; it has always been *he* who took the initiative. One has to forgive these people a lot these days, they are being mercilessly pushed by the times, and live more in train sleepers than at home. I am most happily looking forward to meeting with you. Respectfully,

Stefan Zweig

P.S.   Best regards to Mrs. Strauss

Arosa, Hotel des Alpes
[December 1, 1932 (postmark)]

[Postal card]
Dear Herr Doctor,

   I just barely missed you in Strasbourg and Zurich.[11] I would have liked to show you half of the second act, which I am now finishing. You will receive it in ten days. I hope you will like it, I am pleased with it. The *Neue Freie Presse* has asked me for a sample from the opera for their Christmas edition. I gave it to them because I believe it would increase the interest in advance, and I presume you have no objections. Don't work too hard, Herr Doctor, on your trip. Respectfully,

Stefan Zweig

Garmisch
December 8, 1932

Dear Herr Zweig,

   Thank you for your kind postcard. But I do not consider it the right thing to publish prematurely parts of your work: in any case, two years too soon. Especially an opera libretto! It cannot be judged even by opera experts if they have not heard the music that goes with it. I speak from twenty-five years of experience. Least of all the *Neue Freie Presse*, which always wants to squeeze out contributions from me too, and then turns around and pays me back with rudenesses by Herr Korngold.[12] That would truly mean pearls before . . .

I have never complained to the paper, but to pamper it with special tidbits is something that fine paper has not earned from me.

Please withdraw your contribution at once.

At Christmas I shall be in Rome, early January in Naples (Hotel S. Carlo). After January 10 I'll immerse myself in Sir Morosus.

Best wishes, always respectfully,

Dr. Richard Strauss

Garmisch
December 16, 1932

My dear Herr Zweig,

"The second bar was also a success!"[13] The original and poetic ending is particularly felicitous! My only doubt, after repeated readings, concerns the too-protracted scene between Morosus and Aminta, both before and after the wedding. Maybe you could think about (no hurry) how these discussions could be shortened, cleansed of all incidentals, and reduced to the four main motifs:

1. genuine shyness, based on sympathy,
2. pretended hesitation on the part of Aminta,
3. the bold suitor Morosus,
4. the old man, hesitant and shaken by sincere sympathy for Aminta.

I will not for now botch things by making cuts myself; you, the poet, must try to reduce these scenes to a minimum of words. Setting words to music lengthens even the most precise text. If you could do these revisions for me, I'll then be able, while I am composing, to compare the revised version with the original longer one, from which I then can take whatever additions I might need for the music.

I am still considering whether to opt for *recitativo secco* or for spoken dialogue for the many fast-spoken scenes, especially by the barber. I am afraid *recitativo secco* is not my cup of tea; its diatonic and harmonic Mozartian simplicity does not fit my musical style. What do you think about it?

At any rate, my heartfelt thanks for your brilliant Act II. Best wishes, also from my wife to you and your ladies, always respectfully,

Dr. Richard Strauss

P.S.   Your *Marie Antoinette* is a wonderful, highly interesting book and will be very successful!

Salzburg, Kapuzinerberg 5
December 19, 1932

Dear Herr Doctor,

I am answering your kind letter by return mail. With a sure touch you diagnosed the sick spot; especially the scene before the wedding is *much* too wordy and slow. I thought that here, where the action becomes serious and human, I should apply to the opera the techniques of explanation used on the dramatic stage. This, of course, was an error. I shall rewrite the scene: terse and as clear as possible. As you can see from my cuts I myself was worried about length. The scene after the wedding I think can be rescued just by tightening up, because it is conceived as *presto, prestissimo*, with the characters running back and forth in confusion, which can partly be mastered as duet-like parallelism. This parallelism is indicated by the "I and I and I and I" versus "Oh, I fool, I fool, I fool." I see this scene as moving very fast, yet not too short, because this domestic thunderstorm is to rage to the end with full force before the (I should hope amused) audience, and Morosus is to emerge from it all exhausted as from a heavy hailstorm. I thought that the lengths here would be offset by bodily movements, by the steady *accelerato,* but a few cuts will be wholesome. Still, the first scene, in *lento,* has to be completely rewritten, I feel that myself.

May I now permit myself some comments about the recitative. I think that a heroic theme (Orpheus, Elektra) or a lyrical theme (Tristan) demands composing throughout the entire opera. But in a light opera, with its lively mixture of moods, and, in our instance, continuous scenic-dramatic excitement, a respite from the singing and full orchestration would afford the listeners some happy relaxation and permit them to savor the comedy mood more fully. However, for the *accompagnamento* I do not think of Mozart playing the clavicord—that would smack a little of lavender and pseudo history—but I visualize a very light accompaniment with individual instruments, never more than a few bars of thematic figuration; I am thinking of instruments accented sharper than the clavichord, such as the flute, saxophone, drum, pipes, the violin—a *modern* scansion. I believe here is an opportunity to accomplish something entirely new—something closely akin to your personal idiom of brief illustrative phonetics, a new design, a contemporary musical accenting of the old recitative; this design could have a slightly ironical note, as if the musicians were *playing* with the music during the recitative. I don't know whether my fantasizing makes sense to you, but I do have the feeling that you, better than anyone else, could show the young how to renew and update such an old technique as the recitative; I am thinking of music mocking the pathos of, say, *The Barber of Seville,* while at the same time illustrating it. I think it might be possible to establish the saucy mood through the music, to put a dash of champagne in it with some sparkling tones—but very lightly, here and there, between sentences; this would result, during the spoken parts, in the audience feeling at times sharply stimulated by the music, without being satiated, so that they would savor the music doubly when it starts flowing again.

To sum it up, then, I visualize an occasional pointed, fine touch of musical accenting of the prose recitative, as if the music were just to report: I'm here. But it does not fully enter the scene, the listener gets a respite from it, at the same time expecting it back again. I have the instinctive feeling that especially *you* might be able to create here an entirely *new* design, something modern in the best sense of the word, and at the same time something light and ironical that in a wonderful mood would infuse into the entire work the message: friends, it's all just fun!

If it suits you, I could come to see you in Garmisch in January for one or two days with my new version and could also change details as you desire them. With many regards for Mrs. Strauss, devotedly,

Stefan Zweig

Salzburg, Kapuzinerberg 5
December 19 [sic], *1932*
[postmarked December 18, 1932]

[Postal card]
Dear Herr Doctor,

I am wondering whether I expressed myself clearly enough. I consider prose dialogue for the less important passages as the most natural form, yet I feel that music should not be *wholly* eliminated from prose dialogue but should be sprinkled over from time to time with an ironic, illustrative spark—otherwise the entry of each instrument will sound like the beginning on an aria. I am thinking of short, pointed, sometimes jingly interferences of the music in the spoken dialogue; the audience should at all times be aware of the orchestra's presence—but merely calling, teasing, chatting during the spoken passages on the stage, and only afterward dominating the scene again fully and in earnest. I have in mind dashes of color from individual instruments and imagine a delightful effect of such discreet, witty illustrations. The orchestra amuses itself, as it were, with butting in, making brilliant asides while the people talk—this would go over as something new, modern, comedy-like.

Devotedly,

Stefan Zweig

Salzburg, Kapuzinerberg 5
December 19, 1932

[Postal card]
Dear Herr Doctor,

Here is something from an entirely different shore. The publisher Knaur is preparing an ambitious biography of Richard Wagner on the occasion of the fiftieth anniversary of his death, a fine book, done by Guy de Pourtales, the biographer of Franz Liszt.[14] The publisher asked me for a foreword for this project. I told him who in my opinion is the only competent authority in our time to say something about Wagner, and that is you.

Knaur is a wealthy and generous publisher—anything offered below 1000 marks for the two pages I would refuse if I were in your position. But 1000 marks for just two pages does seem satisfactory compensation in our wretched time; and you would serve a good cause because there are enough super-Germans who will not permit a Frenchman to love Wagner. This is just a footnote to dissuade you from accepting a lower offer; 1000 marks seems like a nice Christmas present.

I am busy working on the revision. Many greetings from your devoted

Stefan Zweig

Regards to Mrs. Strauss.

Garmisch, Zoeppritzstrasse 42
January 16, 1933

Dear Herr Doctor,

Thank you so much for your missive: now Act II is also completed. Looking forward to Number III. Your visit is welcome at any time. I'll be here until February 7, then a few days in Dresden to conduct *Ariadne* and, for the last time, on the thirteenth, *Tristan*. Have you read Sassmann's handsome book

about Austria?[15] Is his assessment of Maria Theresa justified
or a matter of journalistic sensationalism? With warm wishes,
sincerely,

Dr. Richard Strauss

My wife sends her thanks and regards.

Salzburg, Kapuzinerberg 5
January 17, 1933

Dear Herr Doctor,

Applaud, friends, the comedy is finished, said Beethoven on
his deathbed. I am saying it at a more felicitous moment. Here is
Act III, complete except for the Italian aria, for which I have to
find the words. As you see, everything is kept tight, especially the
court scene, which I did not want to have so stupidly crude as in
Ben Jonson, where confessed impotence represents the main joke.
Please tell me all your wishes, and may the whole work please
you—that it will be successful, I do not doubt. With regards to
Mrs. Strauss, devotedly,

Stefan Zweig

P.S.   I am leaving to your musical judgment whether the last
scene might be used earlier (as I indicated in the text), so that the
opera would end with the barber's words: "And now we are
finally gone." Or whether we should end in the present form, with
Morosus' monologue. Let your intuition decide; perhaps the
decision will come while you compose.[16]

Garmisch, Zoeppritzstrasse 42
January 24, 1933

Dear Herr Zweig,

Success, also, for Act III: thanks and congratulations! I would
not know what to criticize. Perhaps a few cuts may be needed

during composition. But there is no hurry, nor do we have to decide now about the ending, which so far I find excellent. After the opera is shown to the public, I recommend a three-year world trip to you, or you won't know how to escape libretto-hungry colleagues. I am busy writing some drafts for the first act—it is easy to set to music.

I have just finished reading your *Heilung durch den Geist*, most interesting and written with the same admirable clarity as all your books. I do not know enough of them and I will, therefore, see whether I cannot mooch some of them from friend Kippenberg who—as far as I'm concerned—has you on his (good) conscience. In this way I will fill my library with the missing books.

To return favors, please let me know which piano scores are missing in your library or which of my works you would like to have.

Ja dass ich dich ge- funden, du lie- bes
Kind, das freut mich alle Tage, die mir be- schieden sind.

Once again, a thousand thanks and best wishes,[17] also to your ladies from my wife, your devoted

Dr. Richard Strauss

P.S. About Sigmund Freud we have to talk some time face to face. The notion of Eros being creative in every artist was not so entirely unknown even before him.

Garmisch, Zoeppritzstrasse 42
January 29, 1933

Dear Herr Doctor,

Thank you so much for your fine package: Dr. Kippenberg also sent a gift. Will it suit you if we now draw up a formal agreement for *Die schweigsame Frau?* Let me repeat our oral agreement: for you 25 percent of the royalties from stage productions, 20 percent royalties from the book; also the manuscript of the piano-score draft.

Please confirm briefly your consent, and I'll then send you a contract drawn up by my attorney Dr. Alex Singer in Prague along the lines of my contracts with Hofmannsthal.

I am busily working away on Act I, which I expect to complete as a draft within two weeks. It lends itself splendidly to composing. The passage after page 22 (Carlotta: "I would sing"), I would like to conclude as a trio for the three women (perhaps adding the barber as a counterpoint). But to do this I need a few verses for Aminta expressing sorrow (contrasting them with those of Carlotta and Isotta), about four, addressed to Henry, matching the enclosed melody.[18] Best wishes, sincerely

Dr. Richard Strauss

P.S.   Just had a letter from my son, saying he asked Dr. Singer to write to you about the contract. There is no need for you to answer him, it is sufficient if you acknowledge the above-mentioned agreements to *me*; I shall then take care of the rest.

I believe it will be necessary for you, as a librettist, to join the Association of German Composers in Berlin to insure that you'll receive your share from concert performances of fragments with lyrics of our opera, also from records and movies.

[Munich, January 31, 1933
(postmark)] *

[Postal card]
Dear Herr Doctor,

I'll be in Garmisch tomorrow Wednesday at 10:30 A.M. staying at the Hotel Alpenhof and shall telephone you at 11 to learn when I may call on you during the day. (Please instruct your maid so you need not bother to answer the miserable telephone.) I will then make all required changes on the spot. Best regards to Mrs. Strauss, gratefully,

Stefan Zweig

---

* This was the day on which Hitler took power. Neither Zweig, nor later Strauss, mention it.

Garmisch, Zoeppritzstrasse 42
February 22, 1933

Dear Herr Doctor,

Recently, in Dresden, I read to some of my most intimate friends and colleagues (Reucker, Busch, Fanto etc.*) the first two acts, and they responded with greatest enthusiasm. The enclosed letter was written by one of my most loyal friends;[19] he is the excellent coach of the Dresden Opera, who has tutored the soloists for all my operas there. His suggestion seems worth considering!

I do not have the third act handy (it is being copied), but perhaps this short comment by Morosus at the end would be sufficient: "And I, old fool, almost fell in love"; and by Aminta: "I very nearly became unfaithful to my Henry!" If you take up Engel's suggestion you probably will find a much better phrasing.

The draft of my first act is finished; I am just preparing a clean copy. Good wishes, sincerely,

Dr. Richard Strauss

---

* Dr. Alfred Reucker, general manager; Leonhard Fanto, stage designer; Fritz Busch, director and conductor, all of the Dresden Saxonian State Opera.

P.S.   I am reading with great pleasure your three-in-one *Casanova, Stendhal, Tolstoy.*

I have long been thinking about a cultural portrayal along the lines of the *Meistersinger:* contrasting, through various minnesingers, the Italian (is there an Italian minnesinger?) and the German (Walther von der Vogelweide) art; between them Ulrich von Liechtenstein, the scoundrel, representing or misusing both styles. Do you think that a good opera plot could be invented for this? I believe Gerhart Hauptmann is working on an epos, *Ulrich von Liechtenstein,* which contains plenty of comedy material; he once read the beginning to me. I talked with Hofmannsthal about this, but he did not want to bite.[20]

Would you care to think about this?

> *Salzburg, Kapuzinerberg 5*
> *February 23, 1933*

Dear Herr Doctor,

It's good to know that you are back safely, and busily at work. As for Erich Engel's intelligent letter, I have the old dramaturgic misgiving: a last act should *never* start a *new* motive but only resolve those already started. Aminta is not likely to show an interest in Morosus with all his strongly comical overtones. I believe that the compassionate sympathy, as I was trying to portray it, is sufficient. Besides, the tone of the opera should remain airy, light.

Your idea of a troubadour-minnesinger libretto seems hard to pull off because of the double analogy, *Tannhäuser* and *Meistersinger.* The substantive kinship would remain and would shine through in many situations. I firmly believe that some themes are exhausted by a truly great master for a century and remain untouchable for anybody else.

When you'll have happily finished your work and are looking for new challenges, I might suggest as an ideal opera subject, mixing serious and light facets, and extremely suitable for being set to music, *The Pied Piper of Hamelin,* perhaps in two acts.

The beginning: desperation among the burghers of a German town about the rat plague, devastation, futile remedy efforts by quacks, exorcisings of the devil, grotesque figures—all this half grotesque, and in the manner of German woodcuts. Arrival of the rat catcher, the great charmer and hypnotist, who promises help. The burghers don't take him seriously and thus don't mind granting him the large sum of money (perhaps also a girl) he demands. Now a musical extra: the magic spell of the flute, the slow hissing, whistling, and emerging of the rats from all houses, and his luring the whole pack down to the Weser River where they all drown. Now the jubilant burghers, revelry, dancing, rejoicing for the hero. Then, when he asks for his reward, limp faces, excuses. Finally they threaten him with the Inquisition, trial for witchcraft. Now his revenge—perhaps not, as in the original story, his luring the children as he had the rats before; instead he now *forces* the entire population to ceaseless dancing (a surging, grand motif as in *Elektra*), and a medieval dancing plague begins. I am not quite sure about the end. I see in the subject a German folk opera *par excellence*, colorful, exciting in music and scenery, ranging from the bright-frolicsome all the way to the ghostlike-grotesque, a popular subject, understandable throughout the world.

But for the time being, Sir Morosus is still holding you, Herr Doctor, and he is in good hands with you. I am immensely pleased that the work flows so creatively. I will certainly come to the *Arabella* premiere in Dresden. There you surely will play the whole first act or parts of it to the musical Big Three.

I'll write to your attorney in Prague about the contract as you are requesting. Good wishes, devotedly,

Stefan Zweig

Best regards to Mrs. Strauss.

Salzburg, Kapuzinerberg 5
April 3, 1933

My dear Herr Doctor,

I postponed my trip to Sweden and Norway, and am just letting you know that I am here. I could understand that in these upsetting times* your work is disturbed, as is mine. A few days ago I experienced a special and incredible trouble: Goebbels in a radio talk quoted an infamous passage from the writer Arnold Zweig[21] without using the first name. Now I am having great difficulties getting a timely correction printed. You can imagine how you would welcome it if someone attributed not only the *Fledermaus* to you but also a little sex murder committed by another composer who has the same name as you. Forgive me this forward comment. I just wanted to inform you, in case you should hear about this crazy error. My next few days will be fully occupied with chasing down and correcting this miserable mixup. Best wishes, as ever,

Stefan Zweig

---

* Railroad-workers' strike and parliamentary crisis in Austria; Reichstag fire and Nazi terror in Germany during February and March.

Garmisch, Zoeppritzstrasse 42
April 4, 1933

Dear Herr Zweig,

I have forwarded your desire for "a timely correction," with ample information from me, to my friend Hugo Rasch, music editor of the Berlin edition of the *Völkischer Beobachter*. I am sure he will do everything he can with the highest chief, Rosenberg, to ensure that justice be done to you.

I am doing fine. Again I am busily at work, just as then, a week after the outbreak of the Great War.[22] I am in the midst of Act II. The draft of Act I is now copied in final form. With best wishes, faithfully,

Dr. Richard Strauss

The first page of the draft score for *Die schweigsame Frau*, begun February 16, 1933.

April 5, 1933

My dear Herr Doctor,

Permit me to thank you for your kind letter on behalf of my husband, who received it just before leaving for a short visit to Vienna. He was very happy about its contents. His reference was not meant to cause you, dear Master, special efforts. Now, however, my husband thanks you most warmly.

May the soft spring sun soon shine upon your work, which makes us very happy.

Sincere regards to Mrs. Strauss, grateful and respectful greetings to you, Herr Doctor, your

Friderike Maria Zweig

Salzburg, Kapuzinerberg 5
April 13, 1933

My dear Herr Doctor,

Back from Vienna, let me first thank you for your great kindness and send warm Easter greetings to you and Mrs. Strauss. I am delighted that your work proceeds well; / politics pass, the arts live on, hence we should strive for that which is permanent and leave propaganda to those who find it fulfilling and satisfying. / History shows that it is in times of unrest when artists work with the greatest concentration; and so I am happy for every hour in which you turn words into music, which lifts you above time for the benefit and inspiration of later generations.

I wish you good health and good, joyful ideas in your work. Gratefully,

Stefan Zweig

Salzburg, Kapuzinerberg 5
May 28, 1933

My dear Herr Doctor,

You can imagine how painful it is for me that the closed border*
deprives me of the pleasure of sharing with you the festive
occasion of hearing your new work:[23] the radio will be a poor
substitute. But please believe that my heart and all my good
wishes will be with those in Dresden who happily and enthusiastically are permitted to hear your latest creation; and when
appreciative ovations sound all around you, my own will silently
be there too. Please remember me to Mrs. Strauss and enjoy your
triumph. Devotedly,

Stefan Zweig

---

* Hitler imposed a prohibitive tax of 1000 marks for crossing the border
between Germany and Austria; its primary purpose was to ruin Austria's
economy by preventing German tourists from visiting. Zweig refers to the
closed border again in his letter of August 10, 1934, and Strauss in his letter
of May 21, 1935.

[August 1933]

My dear Herr Doctor,

Let me express once more my thanks and my fascinated admiration! May you continue to enjoy your work—I am not worried
about its success.

For photo copies you might best approach the Munich State
Library; they will no doubt do these reproductions for you with
pleasure and thus relieve you of your concern for the original.

I am immensely looking forward to the *Helena* performance.[24]
I have never seen a more perfect one.

Greetings and thanks, and my respects to Mrs. Strauss. Your
grateful and utterly admiring

Stefan Zweig

The manuscript is now entrusted to Dr. Kerber.[25]

[Bad Wiessee]
September 2, 1933

Dear Herr Doctor,

You may be interested in the enclosed clipping from the
Münchner Zeitung. The paper would undoubtedly accept a
corrective statement. We are taking the waters here and feel fine.
With best wishes,

Dr. Richard Strauss

Salzburg
September 3, 1933

My dear Herr Doctor,

How good of you to remember—thank you very much: **Jakob
Wassermann**, Thomas Mann, Alfred Döblin, and I had publicly
protested against that blacklist months ago, but this is the time
of the big lie.* Since Christmas 1932 I have not published a line,
except a congratulation to my friend Hermann Bahr here in
Austria, and I have not collaborated anywhere. As a precaution I
sent a statement to Kippenberg today, which he can publish at
any time. As you know from my *Fouché*, politics always disgusted
me and I resist as much as possible being forcefully drawn into
other people's games. But one has to keep defending oneself.

I am still thinking with delight about your wonderful composition; I am almost embarrassed, although it makes me proud,
that my words could stimulate you to so much blessed brilliance
and cheerfulness, so much creative youthfulness. With this music
it seems hard to believe that in this year you will be celebrated
not only as master but as patriarch. Well, you will have to accept
it with a smile, while you belie the calendar years by your
creative work.

I hope you and Mrs. Strauss will fully recover at Wiessee. In a
couple of weeks I will go to the Tessin or to Italy to work and to

---

* The Nazis published a list of prominent cultural leaders opposed to
their regime, depriving them of German citizenship and claiming that they
were despoilers of German culture.

seal myself off entirely from the contemporary situation. I then will probably go to South America. By then let us hope the wild passions of present politics will have abated and the arts will have recaptured their old dominance over the spirit for the others and for us. Conserve your strength and allow Mrs. Strauss to watch over you; we are so poor in new music that every day of your undisturbed, joyful creativeness is worth as much to the world as a year of somebody else.

With respects to Mrs. Strauss and ever-new admiration, devotedly,

Stefan Zweig

[*Salzburg,
December 22, 1933 (postmark)*]

[Picture postcard]

Cordial Christmas greetings to Mrs. Strauss and yourself from your devoted

Stefan Zweig

*Garmisch, Zoeppritzstrasse 42
January 21, 1934*

Dear Herr Doctor,

I have not yet thanked you for your New Year's greetings, because I wanted to combine my acknowledgment with the news that the score of the first act is completed. This news I can give you today. I got 140 pages of the score done in 2½ months, although my appointment as Reich Music Chamber President[26] produces a lot of extra work. I believe I should not refuse this task because the goodwill of the new German government in promoting music and theater can really produce a lot of good; and I have, in fact, been able to accomplish some fruitful things and prevent some misfortune. But now I will have to start thinking about new things. My health is still tolerable, and *Die schweigsame Frau,* I hope, will not be my last effort in this life.

Confidentially—I was not expecting too much of *Arabella*. I worked hard on it and now this enormous success, hardly less, so far, than that of *Rosenkavalier*. It is strange. The public is inscrutable. Despite all one knows about the art, one knows least what one is really capable of doing. One is in God's hand. Best thing would be not to think at all, and yet one has to consider: Now what?

What suits me best are South German bourgeois sentimental jobs; but such bull's eyes as the Arabella duet and the Rosenkavalier trio don't happen every day. Must one become seventy years old to recognize that one's greatest strength lies in creating kitsch? But, seriously, don't you have some new, warm-hearted little theme for me?

How are you? What are you working on? This Thursday I will probably conduct *Arabella* in Munich. It would be nice if you could come, even though this won't be a first-rate performance. Well, all the best to you, and greetings to you and yours from my wife and your grateful and devoted

Dr. Richard Strauss

Salzburg, Kapuzinerberg 5
January 23, 1934

My dear Herr Doctor,

Let me first congratulate you on completing the score of the first act, the result of your superb, untiring working capacity. I hope the unparalleled success of *Arabella* has demonstrated to you how much Germany and the world are waiting for your work. Compared with your creative abundance, there is nothing but sterility, and the human race needs music more than ever. May your health hold out. Perhaps the gratefulness of thousands on the occasion of your festive day this year will tire you,[27] but since you have given to so many you will for once have to tolerate their love and appreciation.

I was in London for some time and plan to get back there again in February to work on a book on Maria Stuart, a counterpart to *Marie Antoinette*. Out of curiosity I looked through old Italian opera libretti in the library there, and I found bewitching characters and situations next to quite fatuous ones. I have some plans, and I am writing them down to show you regardless of whether I or somebody else carries them out; at any rate I learned a great deal about craftsmanship and I believe that when the drafts are clearly outlined they will interest you. I would have come to attend *Arabella* in Munich, of course, but now the greatest pull with officials is necessary for an Austrian to get permission to cross the border; let us hope that this absurd situation will not last long; I would come gladly.

In my own mind I have found my way back to my work. There was much I had to ward off. Attempts continue to drag me into political arguments, even by the coarsest means. Political people cannot understand that there are others to whom all aggressiveness and onesidedness is repulsive and who, like Archimedes in his time, even in the turmoil of war merely want to draw their quiet circles. Except for an obituary for my revered friend Hermann Bahr I have not published anything; I am issuing a small book about Erasmus of Rotterdam privately as a birthday gift for Professor Kippenberg.

The Viennese *Arabella* is a splendid performance, and I am already dreaming (cautiously, as is my custom, so a strong jolt won't knock me out of bed) about the music for *Die schweigsame Frau*. I will soon show you drafts for new themes without any intention of directing or persuading you, dear Herr Doctor; I'm just enjoying the pleasure of playing with plans. To dream of the next project while still working on the present one—this provides a pleasant feeling of continuity, of unbroken visions, and it is this feeling in you to which I hope to contribute, as far as is in my modest powers.

I hope Mrs. Strauss also feels well and happy. Your happiness is guaranteed by your work and your inexhaustible creativeness. Devotedly,

Stefan Zweig

Garmisch, Zoeppritzstrasse 42
January 24, 1934

Dear Herr Zweig,

Just a suggestion: Do you have a copy of Joseph Gregor's handsome *Weltgeschichte des Theaters*, published by Phaidon Verlag [1933]? Look up the heading "Theater der italienischen Renaissance" on page 191 and read about comedy. Don't you think you could fashion a nice one-act play from *Calandria*?[28] I have long been anxious to write an act that, in congenial contrast, would complement *Feuersnot* (one hour and 25 minutes) with a comedy overture!

I probably won't conduct in Munich until next week. Best wishes,

Dr. Richard Strauss

Salzburg, Kapuzinerberg 5
[about January 31, 1934]

My dear Herr Doctor,

I reread *Calandria* at once, but I have great doubts. The Renaissance as scenery is hackneyed and almost always leads to conventionalism in stage direction; also double roles present great casting difficulties in the theater, and especially for the opera; besides, it seems to me that especially at this time something is expected of you that is closely tied to the German mind in some form. I thought (vaguely) of Kleist's *Amphitryon*—you surely have it in your library. Here the confusion of persons lies in the same roles, and the female figure is one of the most charming in literature. From this, by slight adaptation, perhaps a high-class musical comedy could be created. The opposing couple could provide the necessary vividness and boisterousness. The text could be used but would have to be loosened up where the language is too coy, too much loaded with Kleistian bombast, and light operatic elements would have to be introduced. Music could clarify (by leitmotifs) what may confuse the audience in the drama—namely that it is not known who is behind the mask, Zeus or the cheated husband. Why don't you take a look at this sublime comedy before I suggest other subjects. Next month, in the British Museum, I plan to read through all libretti Abbate Casti[29] wrote for Pergolese—who, second-class musician that he was, could not do justice to the great charm and the perfect comedy style of these texts. At any rate you will soon hear from your devoted

Stefan Zweig

Many regards to Mrs. Strauss.

Garmisch
February 2, 1934

Dear Herr Zweig,

I suppose you are right about *Calandria*: I am no devotee of Italian Renaissance theater either. Kleist's *Amphitryon* I know well, but that's not my line at all. Yesterday the thought occurred to me whether one could not do a fine one-act festival play ending with the Peace of Constance, 1043, of the Saxon emperor Henry the Third. If you find the idea interesting why don't you read up on it in Leopold Ziegler's fine *Das heilige Reich der Deutschen*, Volume I, pages 113–141.

With best regards, sincerely,

Dr. Richard Strauss

[In the margin]: I am waiting with intense interest for your Abbate Casti.

Salzburg, Kapuzinerberg 5
February 17, 1934

Dear Herr Doctor,

I have just been to Vienna to see Goldoni's *Mirandolina*, wondering whether it could be made into an opera: the setting, eighteenth-century Venice, is charming, the hostess who tempts everybody but whose heart belongs only to one is theatrically a most appealing figure; but the plot is too thin and needs to be enlivened by a counterplot. Perhaps one could show Casanova in person, who is outdone by her. I am now looking for a German adaptation also of Goldoni's other plays, perhaps something can be used. I have other plans too—but in Vienna an artillery barrage* blared into the beautiful days; it was revolting to awake to the horrible reality after experiencing the philharmonic orchestra with Backhaus as Beethoven soloist.

I plan to go to London at the end of the week to study the Italian texts there; that's the only place to find them. I will write to you from there. I also have a certain thought but I need an additional idea. Poor dramatists believe that *one* idea is enough for one play but it is always necessary that two actions meet and dramatically cross.

I am happy to know you are in good health and busy with creative work. Please remember me to Mrs. Strauss. Devotedly,

Stefan Zweig

* Refers to the armed resistance, on February 12, 1934, of the Austrian Social Democratic workers against the clerical-fascist regime of Chancellor Engelbert Dollfuss.

11, Portland Place, London W.1
[mid-May 1934]

[Picture postcard]
Dear Herr Doctor,

I am busy studying old texts here in London, and will write to you soon. Waiting for the London performance of *Arabella*,[30] sincerely,

Stefan Zweig

11, Portland Place, London W.1
May 17, 1934

My dear Herr Doctor,

I waited for the *Arabella* premiere before writing to you. This letter is above all a congratulation because the success of the performance was extraordinary, not only by the measuring stick of the northern climate but truly spontaneous, sincere, and toward the end rising to quite un-English enthusiasm. You know all the artists from Dresden and Vienna. The direction by Erhardt, and also the settings, were much better than in Vienna— clearer, simpler, livelier. Clemens Kraus has long earned for himself the Grand Cross of the Richard Strauss Order. The reviews, as far as I could see this morning, seem to be very positive, and with that you have beaten the beloved master, because *Fidelio* was reviewed here rather unfavorably as a "novelty." I read with my own eyes, in the year 1934, that *Fidelio* is a "soporifique," dull, and tedious. May the Lord forgive them, they know not what they write. I was all the more pleased to see how cordially your opera was received. Life has been good to you—fight and resistance during your youth, your creative power undiminished up to your mature years, and success that becomes a matter of course. You can imagine how happy the latter makes all those who are sincerly devoted to you.

I expect to be in Salzburg at the end of July or in August, and then would like to suggest some projects to you. None are entirely clear to me but I will bring some ideas along that may stimulate you. My life here is quiet. I work a great deal in the library on my book about Maria Stuart. Despite strenuous efforts by people to rope me in, I have succeeded in remaining entirely aloof from all public discussion and every kind of politics. Shortly I will send you a small book about Erasmus of Rotterdam, a quiet hymn to the antifanatical man who treasured more than anything on earth artistic accomplishment and inner peace—the symbols of my own attitude to life.

The world is getting ready to celebrate you—do not resist the appreciation of millions that will pour out to you at that hour. It is wonderful to see this miserable mass of humanity for once grateful and not envious and hating—enjoy this rare moment.

Best regards to Mrs. Strauss and, again, congratulations from your devoted

Stefan Zweig

Bad Kissingen
May 25, 1934

Dear Herr Doctor,

Warm thanks for your fine, precious letter. For a week I have been meaning to report to you that

"gelungen auch der dritte Bar,"

now I can tell you that I began the score of the second and that I can launch the whole thing in July 1935 for sure.

Can you imagine, the Ministry of Propaganda inquired the other day whether it was true that I am setting to music a text by Arnold Zweig. My son put things straight at once. I recently referred to the subject when talking with Dr. Goebbels, and my son commented that as early as last fall you complained to the *Völkischer Beobachter* that you keep getting mixed up with Arnold Zweig who is not even a relative of yours. I then asked Dr. Goebbels whethere there are any "political objections" against you, to which the minister answered no.

Well, we won't have any troubles with Morosus; I am pleased that you wrote they could not "rope you in." All efforts to relax the stipulation against Jews here are frustrated by the answer: impossible as long as the outside world continues its lying propaganda against Hitler.

Don't you think that Achilles Disguised would make for an appealing one-act show with ballet?[31] (I forgot from which island Odysseus takes Achilles back.) Cherubini already put this theme to music as a ballet. I hope to see you in Salzburg in August. Warm thanks for your good wishes and best regards, also from my wife, your always devoted

Dr. Richard Strauss

Until July 15 alternately in Dresden (Hotel Bellevue) and Berlin (Hotel Adlon).

11, Portland Place, London W.1
June 17, 1934

My dear Herr Doctor,

I sincerely hope that you managed to survive the festivities without getting exhausted and the gratitude of the whole world was a happy experience for you after all. Now the other, greater pleasure begins for you: your creative work. Today I have to report to you a small mishap. Finally, by chance, I happened on an opera theme that seemed ideal to me, but our time makes it impossible: Grillparzer's *Jewess of Toledo*. The king who, because of his love for a stranger, forgets the war; the childlike girl who does not understand her fate; her death—the story has everything, the lyrical, the romantic, the tragic elements, and at the same time the crossing of three cultures, Spanish, Moorish, Jewish; it's a unique setting combining all these elements.

I know that this subject is taboo these days. And so I am wondering whether it could not be transposed into another setting. I don't think there is such a part on the German opera stage: the child-girl, who unconsciously and in an entirely playful and bewitched way, exerts such magic and fashions destiny without knowing it. A figure of this type, in general, would be most attractive; I do not know, for example, whether the figure of Saint Genoveva has ever been used operatically. If not, I see a possibility here, because Genoveva is both a lyrical and dramatic figure, a heroine of suffering—and I believe, without presuming to be a judge on this, that your real strength lies precisely in this conjunction of the lyrical and the dramatic. Such a German fairy-tale, lyrically animated, dramatically gripping, simply and clearly presented, would seem ideal to me today. In your operas the figure of the suffering heroine is still missing—of the woman who vanquishes destiny by her goodness. Perhaps the rigid opera form would have to be adjusted here into a kind of sequence of scenes, as if one were reading a book of woodcuts page by page. And how appealing are also the secondary figures—the duke, an Othello; Golo, an Iago; and the other women. I am going to draft something.

Let me make another suggestion. Here at Regent's Park has been, for about a year, the world's most ideal open-air theater; capacity of 5,000 persons, a jewel in the green, a bewitching stage. Presented are mostly Shakespeare and ballets, and with a charm hard to imagine. The orchestra is covered by greenery, so that the music seems to be coming from the sky. I was there again yesterday; they played Milton's *Comus,* with music and dance. And so it occurred to me—here and nowhere else would be an ideal stage for *Ariadne auf Naxos.* Nowhere else could she achieve such a magic effect. The director of Covent Garden, Dr. Erhardt, enthusiastically agreed. So I thought, if you were to suggest this to Sir Thomas Beecham it could be done, and a work would be rescued for England and the world that is not sufficiently known here (and elsewhere). I know Sir Thomas Beecham slightly, but hardly enough to make the suggestion; perhaps you know a way. But please believe me: *Ariadne* would be enchanting on an open stage, the ideal outdoor opera, and perhaps for the first time ideally staged.

This, then, I would like to suggest. I am somewhat skeptical about the Achilles project—already with *Die aegyptische Helena* you had to discover that the classical characters which we take for granted no longer exist for today's nonhumanistic audiences. All brilliance associated for us with those names is dull for those people, and they are not even ashamed of their ignorance.

As soon as I see more clearly, Herr Doctor, you will hear from me. Respectful greetings to Mrs. Strauss. In loving admiration, devotedly,

Stefan Zweig

11, Portland Place, London W.1
July 21, 1934

My dear Herr Doctor,

I had been looking forward so much to welcoming you on the occasion of your first visit to Salzburg on July 28, but my American publisher, whom I absolutely have to see, unhappily does not get here until July 27 so that I could not get to Salzburg in time. But it is almost certain that on August 12, when you conduct there the second time, I will have the great pleasure of welcoming you. Perhaps I could then suggest some projects to you that might be of interest to you, *even if I were not to work on them myself.* I only wish to serve your eminent art.

I hope to bring with me all my good London humor, because I, too, have completed the most difficult part of my work, which has kept me busy here for months. I probably shall take a vacation combined with a lecture tour to South or North America while your creative work will continue without letup. It seems to me the younger generation is lazier than the older.

My latest book, on Erasmus of Rotterdam, will meanwhile have reached you. I apologize for having it sent to you without a dedication, but it would have been too cumbersome to send the copy to London first. The book appears now in a prepublication edition for close friends only; the regular edition is to appear next year on the occasion of the four-hundredth anniversary of Erasmus' death.

With best regards to Mrs. Strauss, and with admiration, sincerely,

Stefan Zweig

11, Portland Place, London W.1
July 26, 1934

I presume that the unfortunate events * will prevent you from coming to Salzburg now. A British newspaper here ran a story about difficulties with *Die schweigsame Frau,* and a journalist tried unsuccessfully to interview me. You may rest assured that I will do nothing on my part that would give rise to speculations or discussions. I consider silence and aloofness as the required course: we have our work to do and it is not to provide newspapers with gossip. Eventually things always get straightened out. Only those

---

* Chancellor Dollfus was murdered by two Nazis the day before, July 25.

people whose own affairs are of no interest meddle with the
affairs of others. ✒

   I felt I had to say this, Herr Doctor. You can trust me and I
will never be forward enough to get you into a controversy. It is
sad that times continue to be so restless. Here in England I have
found the people's composure, fairness, and restraint truly
refreshing. Devotedly,

Stefan Zweig

Kindly convey my respects to Mrs. Strauss.

Garmisch
July 26, 1934

Dear Herr Zweig,
   Thank you for your fine and kind letter. After the exertions
of this spring I will be unable to come to Salzburg and regret to
have to cancel my visit.[32] But before you leave for America I have
to see you and choose among your new plans. Will you return via
Munich? After August 6 (until then I will be in Bayreuth[33]) I
will be glad to meet you there any time. Best regards, gratefully,

Dr. Richard Strauss

My wife returns your kind regards with thanks.

Bayreuth/Bavaria
Haus Wahnfried
August 2, 1934

Dear Herr Doctor,
   Thank you so much for your fine second letter. In strictest
confidence: You were shadowed in London and your magnificent
conduct has been found "correct and politically beyond reproach."
Please don't let anyone distract you from your attitude and

everything will turn out all right with *Die schweigsame Frau.*
Everything else when I see you. When and where?

After Sunday I will remain in Garmisch. With warmest wishes,
loyally and gratefully,

Dr. Richard Strauss

Klosters, Hotel Weisskreuz
August 10, 1934

My dear Herr Doctor,

Your kind letter reached me here where I am staying for a few
days, till Wednesday, before briefly going to Salzburg and then
to Vienna. Meanwhile I have been chagrined to see how fatuously
your (long previously announced) cancellation has been played
up as a political move. Well, this will pass too; one has to make
allowances for the general excitement.

Do I need to say what an honor, what a pleasure it would be
for me to meet with you soon? Permit me to be candid—to be
honest is always best. I don't want to go to Germany at this time. I
am not afraid—except of silly gossip. Perhaps it would be said
that I was surrendering to those in power, that I had traveled to
Germany to achieve God knows what. It could trigger one of those
disgusting newspaper speculations that neither of us wants for
reasons of integrity and also in the interest of our work. Nowadays
it is being "noted" and commented on if an Austrian writer
travels to Germany, and I want to feed the journalists' imagination
as little as possible.

I am sure you agree with me in your heart, so perhaps it will
not appear unseemly to you when I suggest that we meet let's say
in Ehrwald. For you, this is a short jaunt by car, not a real
journey (which I would never have the audacity to suggest to you);
you could undoubtedly cross the border without having to pay
the thousand marks; besides, it is closer for you to go there than
it would have been to Munich. I could be there any day that you
would indicate three days in advance by wire either between the
fifteenth and eighteenth, or again at the end of August, beginning
of September, after I have returned from Vienna. You won't

regard me as forward, will you, for suggesting the place—I must think that it would be easiest that way, since you frequently go on little trips in that area.

The fate of *Die schweigsame Frau* has never worried me: the essential has been done, the work. Everything else will get straightened out. After all, Mozart's *Don Juan* is still held in esteem today, although the noble librettist Da Ponte was an honest to goodness fellow tribesman of good old Shylock of Venice, which did no harm to the work nor to its continued acceptance in Germany.

I was worried to hear about Mrs. Strauss's operation. I hope the last trace of discomfort is gone and that she is her own self again. With unshakable devotion,

Stefan Zweig

Can be reached by wire until the thirteenth at Klosters (Switzerland), Hotel Weisskreuz; thereafter Salzburg, Kapuzinerberg 5.

[Wire from Garmisch, August 11 or 12, 1934] Stefan Zweig, Hotel Weisskreuz, Klosters. At what hour can I meet you Thursday or Friday, Ehrwald, Hotel Grüner Braum? Regards, Strauss.

[Wire from Garmisch, about August 14, 1934] Stefan Zweig, Hotel Weisskreuz, Klosters. Will arrive Friday in Salzburg for *Elektra*.[34] Hope to meet you there. Regards, Strauss.

Garmisch
August 28, 1934

Dear Herr Doctor,

Gratefully remembering the stimulating hours I was allowed to spend with you in beautiful Salzburg, let me report to you that Heinrich II did, in fact, build the Bamberg cathedral. Hence your suggested cathedral building would be available for world peace.

That is all I have been able to find in the encyclopedia so far, because my history books are in Vienna.

I am now impatiently waiting for further news from you, first the translations of the three Casti operas, then your drafts for them. A parody of the old Roman Englishmen and politicians could be most amusing and "noncontemporary." With best wishes, also to your ladies, sincerely

Dr. Richard Strauss

Vienna
August 21, 1934

Dear Herr Doctor,

My wife tells me by telephone about your kind letter, which I will get here tomorrow. Meanwhile I am writing to you about the festive one-act play: [35] I have thought about it a great deal and would here like to give you the outlines of a plan. I would like to combine three elements: the tragic, the heroic, and the humane, ending in a hymn to international conciliation and to the grace of creativeness, but I would like to leave out emperors and kings and make everything anonymous.

Let me explain the scenes of my plan.

The time: the last year of the Thirty Years' War. The place: the interior of a German fortress under Swedith siege. The commander of the fortress has vowed not to surrender it to the enemy as long as he is alive. The commander laying siege has vowed not to give pardon. Misery reigns in the town below the fortress. The mayor pleads with the commander to surrender the fortress. Town folk enter, various voices express want, fear, hunger (individual voices, intermingled voices, mass scenes). The commander does not yield. He has the people, who curse him, thrown out by force. Alone with his officers and soldiers, he admits he can no longer hold the fort. But he is not going to surrender it, he will blow it up. He gives everybody permission to go down to the town and ask pardon of the enemy, but he would not. Now a few individual scenes (terse, but each sharply profiled). Some leave, some stay, depending on their characters.

Heroic-tragic mood among those that stayed behind.

A religious scene. The commander's wife appears. He orders her to leave without telling her what he intends to do. She guesses his plan. Strong scene. She makes no effort to dissuade him because she knows his vow. But she does not leave. She stays with him— this is the lyrical element—to die with him.

Preparations to blow up the fortress. Final farewells, all embrace. The fuse is prepared. It is lit. Total silence.

There—a cannon shot. Everybody jumps up. The commander expects a charge. The fuse is extinguished. They prefer to die in open battle. But no second cannon shot. All wait, surprised, confused.

A moment of new strong suspense.

There, from the distance, from a neighboring village, a bell (far away) sounding in the silence. Then a second one from another village. Then, still far away, a third. The sound of a trumpet. It is announced that an envoy bearing the white flag of truce is on his way. Then more and more bells. And, suddenly, from below, the cry: peace. Peace has been concluded. The bells sound stronger and stronger and fuse with the jubilant shouts of the (invisible) town people.

The envoy appears. Peace has been concluded at Osnabrück. The enemy commander asks to greet the fortress commander. The latter agrees. A scene of awakening. Again and again the bells sound, flooding the scene like organ music.

The enemy commander appears. The two glower at each other. Each had vowed to destroy the other. Gradual softening of the tension. They step closer to each other. They join hands. They embrace.

The town people come rushing in, cheer the commander. He addresses them: Everybody is to take on a task. Reconstruction and conciliation. Everybody responsible for everybody else. Some voice their agreement. One representative of the various social

classes after another says a few words. And from all this grows, step
by step, a grand chorus in which all tasks and accomplishments
of world peace, as they concern the people in all walks of life, are
glorified; in the finale the chorus unfolds into a mighty Hymn to
Brotherhood.

This, then, is my plan. The idea of international peace can
always be dismissed as pacifist, but in this example it seems to me
to be in a heroic framework. I would leave everything anonymous,
no names for the town or the commander—everybody is thought
to be gestalt, symbol, and not a specific individual.

Now a third matter. I do not mind *at all* if you pass this plan on
to someone else—Rudolf Binding could do it, for example—to
save you all cursed political bother. I am not prompted by reward,
glory, literary honor; it is my pleasure to serve a man whom I
have admired since childhood as the living symbol of music. I
shall be just as pleased if somebody else carries out my suggestions—all that's important is that your creativeness finds the
strongest stimulus to unfold.

If the material in this form does not please you, please let me
know *frankly*; perhaps I can find a better formulation. For the
other materials I will go to the library today. Respectfully,

*Stefan Zweig**

---

* For a response to this letter, see Strauss's reply of September 21.

[*Vienna
August 23, 1934 (postmark)*]

[Postal card]
Dear Herr Doctor,

I am just studying Abbate Casti. The small piece *by itself* is
not usable but could easily be adapted. Delightful is the title,
Prima la musica, poi le parole, "First the music, then the words,"[36]

which, in any case, ought to be retained for this light comedy; also some details. I will write more when I have Vienna behind me. Sincerely,

Stefan Zweig

Regards to Mrs. Strauss.

Garmisch
August 24, 1934

Dear Herr Doctor,

Thank you so much for your card and fine letter. Your draft for the festival play is excellent. In formulating it, may I ask for utmost brevity and conciseness: the talks by the individual persons—people, officers, soldiers—if possible in no more than four lines. Please take a brief look at the *Lohengrin* libretto in this respect: so few words and yet the opera takes four hours. Of course, I would consider only you as the writer.

But for strategic reasons it might be wise, in case we should again collaborate on one or more works, not to say a word to anyone. If anyone asks me, I say: *I am not working on anything now, I have no libretto.* In a few years, when all projects are finished, the world probably will look different.

Prima la musica, poi le parole is excellent. I am impatiently waiting for both books. I finished the score for the second act today. The whole work will be ready by the end of October. Then I will be unemployed. With best wishes and thanks, loyally,

Dr. Richard Strauss

11, Portland Place, London W.1
Presently at Baden near Zurich
[September 1934]

Dear Herr Doctor,

For a few days I have been in "your" Baden; tomorrow I will continue my journey to England; I met Professor Kippenberg here but I did not even tell *him*, whom I know to be a devoted friend of yours, a single word about future plans. I know how to keep quiet in a world in which every word leads to misunderstandings; the situation is complex enough and I do not want to complicate it further by indiscretions. You can rest assured on this point.

For the next six to eight weeks I will be busy with a historical work;[37] after that I'll start the project in earnest and will soon, before the new year which finds you "unemployed," submit some material to you that I hope you will find stimulating. In the meantime you are busy finishing the score. I am not worried about the fate of your work; at a time that creates so much noise and commotion and so little music, your accomplishment will not long remain hidden. All true works of art have the built-in strength to overcome resistance; I am not timid, I just refrain from doing anything that would increase the difficulties.

Please give my regards to Mrs. Strauss. Sincere wishes for your work and yourself, devotedly,

> *Stefan Zweig*

> *11, Portland Place, London, W.1*
> *Presently at Folkstone*
> *September 13, 1934*

My dear Herr Doctor,

Let me give you a sign that I think constantly and with good feelings about your work plans. Perhaps there is a happy way out of the difficulties of the present time. Forgive me for pleading today the case of a much respected friend more strongly than that of my own. I have long had on my mind the extraordinary dramatic festive play *Opferspiel* by Robert Faesi,[38] the most distinguished Swiss poet, a true poet indeed. The theme of this festival play is the celebrated episode *Bürger von Calais*, which Rodin cast in bronze. (The national overtones of the subject are kept low.) Faesi interprets the theme as a heroic drama at the highest spiritual level and with the action in sharp profile.

But the form of the drama is not suitable for music, hardly for the stage even. The author himself, in a notation on the last pages, drafted a "simplified stage version." But I know his admiration for you and have no doubt that he would rework the play for music and reduce it to one-tenth. I consider the material simply as a fortunate chance for musical treatment: the seven burghers with their different voices and characters, the elevated world of the king, the dark mass of the people, the sharply defined motions, the exciting events, and at the end a truly magnificent rise from the tragic element into salvation with a simultaneously religious, humane, and heroic upturn.

I shall send you the play. Please read it, but *not* for details and words—these would all have to be changed and cast into a different style—but for the plot and the theme and the musical potential. I believe that something could be made of this; three-quarters could be omitted, such as the entire prison act and many details. Robert Faesi, one of the best poets as I said, would undoubtedly be enthusiastic about the task. Please do not interpret my suggesting a friend as an attempt to withdraw from you; it just occurred to me, almost as an inspiration, that here as nowhere else an opera on a high and spiritual level is, as it were, *predesigned*, and so beautiful that I could never invent anything better. Perhaps you would permit Faesi to discuss this with you some time in person. He is a professor at the University of Zurich, but plans to be in Munich soon and would be agreeable to all your suggestions, I am sure. In the meantime I am not forgetting the other plans, which I only set aside in my mind in favor of this superior one. Best regards to you and Mrs. Strauss, faithfully and respectfully,

Stefan Zweig

Garmisch
September 21, 1934

Dear Herr Zweig,

Faesi's *Opfergang* is beautiful poetry, rich in important thoughts, using noble language, and with moving scenes. But it does not have what it takes for a good effective opera. The plot by itself is not interesting enough for the composer and the public; what is best in it (from the literary viewpoint) would have to be cut. Thank you so much for your *Opfergang*: if you don't mind, I'll stick with Stefan Zweig.

Thinking about your *24. Oktober 1648*,[39] I had what I think is a good idea today. Your draft (the structure is excellent) seems a little too plain and straight to me and lacks an inner conflict, which would make it more interesting.

What would you think of a love affair between the wife of the fortress commander (she is twenty years younger than her husband who is about fifty) and one of the commander's lieutenants, in this way:

Beginning of the opera: Flirtatious scene between the woman who loves the lieutenant without as yet being aware of it, and the lieutenant who has not yet confessed his love to her; in this scene the tragic situation of the fortress and the people inside is explained.

At the end of the scene the commander enters; he has an inkling about how the two feel about each other. Then the scene with the mayor and the people could follow; and the commander's decision never to surrender the fortress and to permit everybody to leave who does not wish to stay.

The woman senses that her husband is prepared to die.

Thereafter a major scene between the woman and the lieutenant. She tries to persuade him to leave the fortress and thereby betrays her love. Yet, after a passionate outburst and a stormy embrace she decides to stay and die with her husband, as long as her paramour is saved.

She implores him to leave. He departs without making a definite decision. He wavers between his love for the woman whom he does not want to desert, his soldier's honor, his wish to live—I can see a beautiful and colorful scene here.

Now follows the scene between the commander and his wife, in which she tells him about her decision to stay with him—made more pointed by the fact that the commander is becoming increas-

ingly aware of the love situation between his wife and the
lieutenant, and is moved by her double sacrifice.

After this the story follows your draft until the end, when in
the mood of general happy relief the love between wife and
lieutenant becomes apparent; the lieutenant could perhaps kneel
before the wife and kiss her gown in an upsurge of enthusiasm.

The commander shoots himself: the sacrifice, which he first
meant to make in order to redeem his officer's honor, is now made
in human renunciation of the beloved and honored wife, opening
for her the road to join her lover.

This briefly is the rough idea offered for your comments. Did I
write to you that Dr. Goebbels told me the Reich Chancellor
approved the performance of *Die schweigsame Frau*? I am now
negotiating with Dresden about the necessary guarantees, also on
the part of the Saxony government, and about safeguards (so far
as possible), such as Dr. Goebbels has most readily promised. I
am postponing my final, definitive decision, whether to come out
with this work next summer and in Dresden, until November when
I will *personally discuss* the matter and all its consequences with
Dr. Goebbels in Berlin. In the meantime I will finish the score[40]
and ask you urgently to continue work on both our new drafts.
With best regards, sincerely,

> *Dr. Richard Strauss*

> *11, Portland Place, London, W.1*
> *October 3, 1934*

My dear Herr Doctor,

Forgive me for not answering your kind letter until today: I
was unable to do so for a few days. I have thought about your
plan carefully. But I find the tie-in between the heroic element
and the love episode a bit too operatic in the unfortunate sense
of the word. To me, a certain conventional romanticism is un-
avoidable here, which automatically will influence the music. I
always feel uncomfortable when men representing heroes burst
into an amorous aria; this seems to be the ideal mixture for the

audience because it has been used so many times. But my instincts are against it.

So far I have only taken some notes because I am all wrapped up in work until the end of November. But in December I'll chance a draft: I now see more liveliness in the tragic-heroic material than is apparent in the plot. The wife also has a considerable part, beyond all erotic aspects: in the main scene, which I can see in all details, when at the moment of imminent death suddenly from the distance the first bell begins to break the silence, then the second, the third, before the men under siege understand this message of peace—from this moment until, entirely engulfed by the roar of bells, they *comprehend* what has happened, one messenger after another comes, each with a stronger message, then all the people rush in—all this seems to be a grandiose situation with all conceivable possibilities. Then follows the great scene between the former opponents still stuck in their hatred, the voices of the wife and priest tune in soothingly, former hatred dissolves in mutual respect, and then, after this reconciliation between the men (which is to be truly moving), the grand fugue develops, the hymn to peace, to work, to life itself.

This sober recounting of the contents hardly reflects the possibilities for the utmost tensions contained in the plot: revolt, despair, determination, then the separation of the soldiers into those who volunteer to stay and those who do not have the strength —all conceivable gradations. Then the woman's determination to sacrifice herself, the religious fervor of the sacrifice, the moment before the gate—and, rising from all this, clearer and clearer the bells' message of salvation, the *miracle* of salvation at the last moment. By praising the plan I do not wish, so help me, to persuade you, Herr Doctor; nothing could be worse than to exert pressure when the final conviction is missing. But when I can breathe a bit I will work out the center section in a rough draft just to give you a sample of how I approximately visualize it; you are, of course, not obliged to say yes or no.

I was glad to hear that your opera is now overcoming the

difficulties—the true victory was the internal one—that you happily
completed the work, that the blessing of creating was bestowed
on you so magnificently. Covent Garden here is in great expecta-
tion, and I am convinced that your work, like your other works,
will belong to the whole world.

Kindly convey my regards to Mrs. Strauss. Sincerely,

Stefan Zweig

Garmisch
October 10, 1934

Dear Herr Zweig,

You are undoubtedly right, and the material as you describe it,
is certainly purer and greater, but please don't forget I have to
compose it and it has to express feelings which kindle in me
emotional music. The motives of despair, heroism, weakness,
hatred, reconciliation, and so on do not, I'm afraid, inspire enough
music in me that truly goes to the heart. To be sure, my suggestions
were operatic, but where does the kitsch end and the opera begin?
Of course, I must not try to persuade you but I do have the feeling
that the plot is a little too straight; it lacks contrast, the erotic
element, figures expressing weakness, indecision. Perhaps you can
reconsider and think of something better, less kitsch, which
meets my doubts and wishes.

The score of the third act will be ready in a few weeks, and then
I'll have nothing to do.

How about Casti?

It would be nice if I could get both books, the cheerful and the
serious one, at the same time. From November 28 to December 1
I will be in Amsterdam, Amstel Hotel. I will conduct *Arabella*
there on November 29 and December 1. Could we meet there?
With best wishes, gratefully,

Dr. Richard Strauss

11, Portland Place, London, W.1
October 23, 1934

My dear Herr Doctor,

Thank you so much for your good letter. The scenario for the little one-act comedy is finished. I shall send it to you before I formulate the final version.

Today just a bit of information. A foreign newspaper tells a stupid story about Toscanini having made sarcastic and derogatory comments about you at a party held in my honor here in London. How *stupidly* this episode is *invented* (it appeared under the headline "Toscanini's hat shop"),[41] is evident by the fact that I *never* saw Toscanini in London; he has not been here for a year and, of course, he never made a comment like that. Unfortunately, there are always people inclined to draw persons who are a thousand times superior to them into a smear campaign. Now, I do not want you to be annoyed about Toscanini, if you hear about this idiotic fabrication; as far as I know he *never* made such a silly joke, certainly not in my presence, since he knows my devotion to you. The world, indeed, has hatred enough. Again and again these repulsive diatribes!

I very much hope to get to Amsterdam by the end of November. In the meantime I shall send you the first, informal sketch. Hurriedly, with devotion,

Stefan Zweig

11, Portland Place, London W.1
[November 1934]

Dear Herr Doctor,

All this time I had hoped to be able to go to Amsterdam, but I cannot make it. I have to go to Paris for conferences and then soon, for a short time, to America. Before I go I will send you the draft, which somebody else will be able to work out. I am only now about to finish my large book on Maria Stuart. Then I'll be free and uncommitted, then everything will succeed better and with élan. I was happy to hear from friends about your conducting in Berlin [42]—may your wonderful vitality remain unimpaired. You'll hear from me *very* soon. My respects to Mrs. Strauss, faithfully,

Stefan Zweig

Garmisch, Zoeppritzstrasse 42
December 21, 1934

Dear Herr Doctor,

In Joseph Gregor's *Weltgeschichte* I read on page 359 that Cardinal Richelieu wrote a play *à clef*, titled *Europe*, that ends with a reconciliation between *Germanique* and *Francion*. *Austria* comes off very poorly. Wouldn't it be a historical joke to show this play now in the Berlin Staatstheater?

Please read it at the London library and let me know whether it has been translated and adapted by anybody (?), whether it could be by you, as an Austrian perhaps anonymously, and whether it is performable, possibly as a matinee for invited guests.

When will I hear from you otherwise? I kill the boredom of the Advent season by composing an Olympic hymn for the proletarians—I, of all people, who hate and despise sports. Well, Idleness Is the Root of All Evil.

We are well. Do you plan to stay in London all winter? All the best and a happy new year, faithfully,

Dr. Richard Strauss

Garmisch, Zoeppritzstrasse 42
January 10, 1935

Dear Herr Zweig,

Along with my best wishes for the new year my humble inquiry when I may expect another fine present from you? Desperately idle, I just composed a short (four minutes) overture for *Die*

schweigsame Frau, entitled "Potpouri,"[43] but now I am really
a fish out of water. [. . .]

Let me soon have good news. Warm greetings, gratefully and
sincerely,

Dr. Richard Strauss

[February 5, 1935]

Dear Herr Zweig,

In the interest of our *Schweigsame Frau* I should like to request
that you withdraw from the International Music Club or at any
rate I recommend that you have your name withdrawn from the
list of *Unio* advisors. Didn't you get my last letter?

When will I get good news? With best regards, sincerely,

Dr. Richard Strauss

February 9, 1935

Dear Frau Zweig,

Thank you for your kind letter. The last letters I received from
your husband were dated London, October 3 and 23. Since then
I regret not to have heard from him. When do you expect him
back? Will he return to London or to Salzburg? I recommend
special attention to my last postal card! With warmest wishes,
sincerely,

Dr. Richard Strauss

Salzburg, Kapuzinerberg 5
February 18, 1935

Dear Herr Doctor,

Just returned from America I find your kind letters, from
which I see that you did not receive my last three letters—one
of them registered. I will inquire at once. In the last one I had

raised, in your interest, the question whether the performance should not be postponed in order to avoid any connection with the events in the musical world (Furtwängler,* and so on) and allow time for a strictly artistic evaluation. A world premiere of an opera by Richard Strauss must be an *event* of the highest artistic significance, not *an affair*. The minds of the musical world are still too upset.

I am surprised about your *Unio* message—I don't even know whether the club still functions; and in no case did that project, which was to advance and popularize opera in small communities from a purely artistic point of view, have anything to do with politics. The program included among its six operas three German ones (one of them *Arabella* by Richard Strauss), so that even the most malicious interpretation could not see in it an attack against Germany; and Toscanini, who signed first, has just opened his symphony orchestra concerts in New York (I heard it myself with admiration) with *Salome's Dance* by Richard Strauss!!! I keep away from politics, and the nice plan foundered, as far as I know, because of financial difficulties. For me to withdraw my name would be a demonstration on my part that would make out an enterprise to be political which never was; a *sacrificio d'intelletto* always causes nothing but harm. You know, Herr Doctor, how important it is for me not to create difficulties in this already complex situation, and I have a clear conscience not to have caused any. But such a withdrawal of my name would *provoke* arguments. I would think it best to let some time go by, then the public itself will *request* your opera instead of the work having to *petition* to be performed by making all kinds of concessions. As ever, devotedly,

Stefan Zweig

---

* The Nazis attacked conductor Wilhelm Furtwängler for opposing the ouster of Jewish members of the Berlin Philharmonic Orchestra and for defending the composer Paul Hindemith, whose music was banned by the Nazis as opposed to their cultural policies. Furtwängler, increasingly *persona non grata*, eventually left Germany for Switzerland.

Scene from the world premiere of *Die schweigsame Frau*

Garmisch
February 20, 1935

Dear Herr Zweig,

Thank you very much for your long-anticipated letter. Concerning your message about the International Music Club I will report to Berlin in writing and in person, but concerning *Die schweigsame Frau* there is nothing to do or postpone now that Hitler and Goebbels have officially approved. Dresden also has made its announcements for June-July, so fate must take its course. But for the future: Should I have the good fortune to receive one or several new libretti from you, let us agree that nobody will ever know about it or about my setting them to music. Once the score is finished, it will go into a safe that will be opened only when we both consider the time propitious.

This being so, will you take the chance of writing something new for me—possibly for my estate? With best wishes, sincerely,

Dr. Richard Strauss

Vienna, Hotel Regina
till March 20

February 23, 1935

Dear Herr Doctor,

I received your kind letter in Vienna. If the performance does not take place until June, some time will have passed, and I can only hope that attention will be focused on the artistic aspect. If only emotions would quiet down!

Concerning new projects, let me write to you candidly. You know my devotion for you, and it alone gives me the right to be straightforward. Sometimes I have the feeling that you are not quite aware—and this honors you—of the historical greatness of your position, that you think too modestly about yourself. Everything you do is destined to be of historic significance. One day, your letters, your decisions, will belong to all mankind, like those of Wagner and Brahms. For this reason it seems inappropriate

to me that something in your life, in your art, should be done in
secrecy. Even if I were to refrain from ever mentioning that I am
writing something for you, later it would come out that I had
done so secretly. And this, I feel, would be beneath you. A Richard
Strauss is privileged to take in public what is his right; he must
not seek refuge in secrecy. No one should ever be able to say that
you have shirked your responsibility. Your grandiose work,
incomparable in the world of the arts, imposes the responsibility
on you not to allow yourself to be limited in your free will and
your artistic choice. Who, beside you alone, has this right today?

I am aware of the difficulties that would confront a new work
if I were to write the text; it would be considered a provocation.
And to work together secretly seems to me beneath your rank, as I
said. I will be happy, however, to assist with counsel anybody
who might work for you, to sketch things out for him—without
compensation, without boasting about it, simply for the pleasure
of serving your great art and in order to show my appreciation
for the fact that you took *Die schweigsame Frau* and created from
it a work of art for the world. I will cooperate with anybody
whom you care to name, without credit or reward. With admiration,

Stefan Zweig

My regards to Mrs. Strauss.

Garmisch
February 26, 1935

Dear Herr Zweig,

Your beautiful letter saddened my deeply. If you abandon me,
too, I'll have to lead from now on the life of an ailing, unemployed
retiree. Believe me, there is no poet who could write a usable
libretto for me, even if you generously and unselfishly were to
"cooperate." My warmest thanks for your magnanimous offer. I
have repeatedly told Minister Goebbels and also Göring that I
have been searching for a librettist for fifty years; dozens of texts
were sent to me, I negotiated with all German writers (Gerhart

Hauptmann, Bahr, Wolzogen, and so on). To find *Salome* was a piece of luck, *Elektra* introduced me to the incomparable Hofmannsthal, but after his death I thought I would have to resign myself forever. Then by chance (is that the right word?) I found you. And I will not give up on you just because we happen to have an anti-Semitic government now. I am confident this government would place no obstacles in the way of a second Zweig opera and would not feel challenged by it if I were to talk about it with Dr. Goebbels, who is very cordial with me. But why now raise unnecessary questions that will have taken care of themselves in two or three years? So I am sticking by my request: do a few more beautiful libretti for me (I will *never* find another writer), and we will keep the matter confidential until we both deem the time right to come out with it. This is not undignified but wise.

I had planned anyway to suggest to Dr. Goebbels that he launch a contest for libretti. We'll see what comes of this. God have mercy on the Herr Minister if he then has to read all those submitted texts.

And so: I'm waiting! But not too long, I hope. Sincerely,

Dr. Richard Strauss

Vienna, Hotel Regina
March 14, 1935

My dear Herr Doctor,

Forgive me for not answering your kind letter earlier. I work day and night proofing my Maria Stuart book, which is scheduled to come out in three weeks. In the meantime I received a communication from the Association of German Playwrights accepting me as a member. Therefore nothing stands in the way, on my part, of the performance [of *Die schweigsame Frau*], for which, I understand, rehearsals are in full swing. Meanwhile I am studying an old Spanish tragicomedy, *Celestina*,[44] which for years I have been considering for an adaptation and which probably could provide the basic idea for an opera. It is the oldest drama of

Spanish literature, older than the works by Calderon and Lope,
and remarkable because it moves on two levels: two lovers, noble,
romantic, in the lyrical tradition, patterned after Romeo and
Juliet; and the lower elements, crude, vulgar; in between, as
mediator, the unique figure of Celestina, a full-blooded matchmaker with an outstanding command of words, a female Falstaff,
juicy, elementary. What is noble, lyrical, tender in the upper
level shown is also with the servants, scoundrels, and scamps, as
in a distorting mirror. This contrast seems to me a most appealing
musical theme—to show love in its noble and crude forms,
romanticism and crass realism mixed as in everyday life. Clearly
such a work can never be translated, only adapted. There is an
adaptation in verse by Zoosmann. Perhaps you could have it ordered
from a library; I do not recall the title exactly, but any librarian
will be able to find it from the title *Celestina,* freely rendered by
Richard Zoosmann. The material could be interesting for you,
I believe, because it encompasses both ends of the spectrum of
expression and because the Spanish coloration is missing on the
palette. In operatic terms, the figure of Celestina would introduce
a new type—a female Falstaff, I cannot say it differently; it is,
boldly speaking, a female buffo role, something unknown, as far
as I know. Perhaps I will be able to suggest something else in
two weeks when I have finished with the corrections of my book
and can think more clearly.

May the collector in me remind you and ask whether I may have
the hand-written draft of the piano score of *Die schweigsame
Frau*[45] now or do you prefer to keep it until after the premiere?
I would not show it to anybody, of course, and I am mentioning
it only because I will be in Vienna for another three weeks and
then probably disappear to Italy.

Good wishes to Mrs. Strauss. Enjoy the beautiful spring before
the hot days of the Battle of Dresden. Devotedly,

Stefan Zweig

Garmisch
April 2, 1935

Dear Herr Zweig,

I had a long talk with the minister and the secretary of state, and both regretted that the performance of a *second* Zweig opera would not be acceptable. I told them that for the well-known reasons you had refused to continue to work for me but that I did not wish to be without work during the final years of my life (which can refer only to the stage because the so-called absolute music has just about come to an end since the Ninth Symphony); that I consider it honorable to let the minister (but nobody else) know that I will continue to compose Zweig texts if I cannot find another librettist, but only in secret; that nobody will know about this (I am asking you, too, for strictest secrecy); and that I will work only for my desk drawer, for my pleasure, for my estate.

In this way I have protected myself. In two or three years, if a new opera is finished by then, we will see what to do next. Upon my suggestion, Dr. Goebbels will launch a contest for German opera libretti; we'll see what comes of it. I expressed my willingness to compose a text *that should prove to be usable for me* (but I don't believe there will be one).

I shall write for *Celestina* at once. This material has possibilities. It's a matter of how to handle it and whether it is possible to create from the mentioned figures characters who interest us as human beings, not merely entertain us, as you succeeded so well in doing with Morosus; and how to avoid the parallel Ariadne/Zerbinetta.

Please continue to think also about the Westphalian peace and the de Casti comedy. Could you get me his *Catilina* to read? Having glorified the Greeks so abundantly, I would like to poke fun at the famous Romans.

I will send you the manuscript of the piano score as soon as the arranger has finished with it. Sincerely,

Richard Strauss

April 6, 1935

Dear Herr Zweig,

I've plowed through *Celestina* twice now. The figure of Celestina is indeed a brilliant *part*, but no more than a part, for a play that is even weaker than [Otto Nicolai's opera] *Die lustigen Weiber* [*von Windsor*]. Or rather, it is no play at all, but a succession of scenes, which, to be sure, are splendid (especially the first ones, with Celestina). Splendid, too, is the character of the matchmaker and, in part, also the characters of the underworld: Crito, Centurio, the three girls, Parmeno.

The lovers are rather conventional, but the love scenes include many beautiful thoughts and precious verses, fine material for a dramatic treatment that still has to be supplied. The upper and lower worlds are much too loosely connected, only at the beginning by Celestina and Parmeno/Ines, Luis/Ines, Sempronio/Elicia, and so on, who never get into direct dramatic conflict with the couple. The parents—a pale version of the Montagues and Capulets—are impossible, at least for the tragic ending, for which there is no reason because Pleberio, from the outset, is inclined to forgive the murder of his brother; hence the parents would have to be treated in a semihumorous vein, because Calisto's misunderstanding (that the murder of his brother is the reason for his not being allowed to marry Melibea) justifies neither the long secretive behavior, nor the flight, let alone the tragic end. The only one who could conceivably be murdered at the end would be Celestina or, possibly, Don Luis. But he, as well as Fabio, would have to be tied much closer to the plot; in a finale of the second act or at the end (as in *Figaro*) everything has to clash.

It does not make sense that the three prostitutes are suddenly out to kill Calisto in the fifth act. Parmeno, seduced by Celestina, would at least have to betray his master. Above all, dear Herr Zweig, from all these excellent single scenes would have to be created a truly integrated plot culminating in a happy ending; and all similarity with the much stronger Romeo and Juliet story would have to be avoided. Do you think this possible? Much previous material is there, but an even half-way interesting plot would have to be invented. For example, Don Luis always talks about his hope to marry rich, but his tale just coasts along as a side issue until he gets murdered by some chance. The Luis/ Ines episode is good. As for Parmenio/Ines, a direct tie with the main story is missing. I wonder whether I express myself clearly. Fabio has no profile either! Could Melibea's assorted suitors not be shown in a great scene at the parents? Or whatever else your vivid imagination whispers to you. You are right: Celestina's part alone is worth the work on this material. But the play must be better than *Falstaff*.

There is plenty of material for charming pieces—trios, sextets; just the connecting link is missing. Let me know soon about your further decisions. Best wishes, sincerely,

Dr. Richard Strauss

Vienna, Hotel Regina
April [12], 1935

My dear Herr Doctor,

Accompanying this letter is an Easter egg for you, which I hatched during my year in London, my *Maria Stuart*. With it I got rid of a rock that burdened my work. I am delighted that you also see elements of an opera in *Celestina*. I like two things about it, first, juicy Celestina herself, who would be something new in the rigid realm of opera figures, a human being who radiates elementary exuberance and mirth; and secondly, the lover who in his unworldliness becomes the victim of those scoundrels. It's true, the plot is too primitive, it must be newly invented, and enlivened, as you say; the only usable part in it is Celestina, who couples the upper ethical-lyrical world so magnificently with the vulgar. I'll think it all over and will jot down a few things on paper, which you then could pass on to somebody

to work on. I repeat that, because of my admiration for you,
I gladly and without reward will counsel anybody, and anonymously will assist anybody who can produce a usable text for you;
this is an honor for me, regardless of any public or material
acknowledgment. In the meantime, the performance of *Die
schweigsame Frau* will disclose the attitude of public opinion
toward my collaboration. I have consistenly never said a word
to any newspaper and will let things take their course. Who can
know today how the public attitude manifests itself. We live in
a time where things change from one week to the next and we will
have to get used to the elimination of the concept of "security."
All one can do is act reasonably and according to one's own
convictions, and this I am determined to do. If I can be useful
to you in the future, it will be because of artistic gratitude and
personal friendship and will have nothing to do with the public,
money, or the law. I am ready to serve in this private sense. Should
the contest turn up something useful, I would still be glad to
make dramaturgical suggestions. The difficulties and—to my
mind—injustices with which I am publicly confronted will never
influence my personal attitude toward you.

Are you familiar with the contemporary writer Lernet-Holenia?
He seems to me just right for a work of high quality. His *Saul*
and his *Alkestis* (already set to music) are the purest creations
we have in German literature after Hofmannsthal and Carossa.
I am going to see him in a few days and would like to suggest to
him that he approach you with a theme. It would be a special
stroke of luck for you, if this noblest of our dramatists (who also
has some feeling for the grotesque) could create something for
you.

Let us hope *Die schweigsame Frau* will soon find her voice now.
Best wishes to you and Mrs. Strauss. Sincerely,

Stefan Zweig

Garmisch
April 12, 1935

Dear Herr Zweig,

My friend Hugo Rasch sent me the enclosed critical comments on the texts of our singing lesson.* I composed the Italian texts precisely as written in the enclosed manuscripts; if you consider changes necessary, please let me know immediately, because the third act is ready for the last corrections.

Let me know soon something interesting about your various plans!

By the way: Do you know the excellent essays by E. Th. A. Hoffmann, *Dichter und Componist* and *Leiden eines Theaterdirektors?* Excellent!

Please let me know your next addresses in good time.

I will be here till April 26, and from the 29th in Kissingen care of Dapper until about May 20. Then until June 11 alternately in Garmisch and Munich, on June 12 in Dresden (world premiere on the 24th). Very best wishes,

Dr. Richard Strauss

* A scene in *Die schweigsame Frau.*

Garmisch
April 13, 1935

Dear Herr Zweig,

Thank you for your fine letter. It saddens me because I sense in it your discouragement about our "time," which is apt to disturb considerably our working together. Your generous offer to help with another librettist is very kind—you know as well as I do that there is no one else. The contest will not produce a suitable libretto, not for me, at any rate; but it will be very important to prove this and it will strengthen my contention. Maybe there will be some talented samples, but it is a long way from there to a truly viable libretto.

Your *Die schweigsame Frau* was incontrovertible proof to me—please stay with me and continue to work with me. The rest will take care of itself. No one will hear about it—in any case, I am protected on all fronts as far as Dr. Goebbels is concerned. If there is no change two years from now, we'll leave the work locked in the desk and we both will at least have had the joy of producing it. And this is the most beautiful part of it all. Nothing wrong with Lernet-Holenia, but there is no more than perhaps one good libretto in three hundred good plans. It requires a very special talent.

If Lernet H. wants to try, I will conscientiously examine what he has to offer. But I expect nothing.

Whatever you "jot down on paper" for me will never be "passed on to somebody to work on," because it is not so much the material that matters, but the kind of person who does this "working on." You know that yourself. So let's forget it. Warm wishes, sincerely,

Dr. Richard Strauss

Hotel Regina, Vienna
April 15, 1935

My dear Herr Doctor,

I was just visited by a lady, a professor from Milan, and studied the Monteverdi readings with her. Herr Rasch turns out to be right on all points. For the *written* form his text is not to be touched; in singing, to be true, most syllables at the end are eliminated in Italian by contradiction. There are variations in the written style, just as we, in German, vary between *andern* and *anderen*. But Herr Rasch's version is definitely the one to be used for printing, not Riemann's.

On page 349/50 it should read, of course, "Comincia." There must have been a typographical error in copying my text: I'm glad this was straightened out.

I assume you received the letter I wrote you two days ago. I hope to see Lernet-Holenia in the next few days. A *noble* writer.

In a hurry (just before the ultimate evil, a dental appointment), sincerely,

Stefan Zweig

Hotel Regina, Vienna
April 16, 1935

Dear Herr Doctor,

Let me hurriedly suggest something I consider wise from a practical standpoint: to include at the beginning or end of the piano score and the full score of *Die schweigsame Frau* the date on which you started the first drafts and when you concluded the work. I would like to do the same in the libretto.[46] *That would easily head off much fatuous argument,* because it would be evident from the date that you started the opera long before the changes in politics. It will save us silly talk and conjecture: by this dating we will say openly when the work and our collaboration started and when you concluded the work. *I hope there is still time to insert it.* Good ideas always arrive at the last minute. I trust you will recognize the usefulness of this small step. Perhaps you will even consider giving scholars the pleasure of more detailed information, such as: first drafts from . . . to . . . Piano sketch started . . . finished . . . instrumentation of first act started . . . finished . . . and so on.

I expect to meet Lernet-Holenia for an extensive discussion next week. I wish he could do some good writing for you. I would love to assist this distinguished man, this noble writer!

Best Easter greetings from house to house, sincerely,

Stefan Zweig

Garmisch
April 20, 1935

Dear Herr Zweig,

I have inserted the dates.

Herr Lernet-Holenia, in a friendly letter, has announced that he will send me two plays, *Alkestis* and *Das Weib des Potiphar*, but I am skeptical.

For the moment I am waiting for your three proposals, *Celestina, 1648*, and de Casti's *Prima la musica, poi le parole*.

Now something else, that I see more vividly before my eyes than ever before: Semiramis. For years Hofmannsthal and I considered Calderon's *La hija del aire* [*Daughter of the Air*].[47] Finally Hofmannsthal declined the project. What's left is a fragment: *Semiramis*, published in the 56th volume of Rupprecht Presse, Munich, sponsored by Heinrich Beck and edited by F. U. Ehmke, spring 1933, 150 numbered copies. If you cannot get it in Vienna, where shall I send you my copy? Please read it, together with Calderon's *La hija del aire*; perhaps you could discuss the idea with Lernet H. I cannot tear myself away from the idea of Semiramis. I am intrigued by the very title and by "hanging gardens"—please don't laugh. The female demon as statesman and general is yet missing in my women's gallery. I have already sketched some themes—the heroic woman! Calderon's verse drama easily yields three splendid acts. (Cosima Wagner once told me: Dear friend, first thing to make sure is that the act finales are right.) Most important question: Which aspects of the Semiramis problem can be made relevant to our contemporary thinking? Audiences nowadays won't go along even with Helena and Menelaos, and those, heaven knows, are modern enough.

I once discussed this with Werfel in detail. He wanted to transplant the Semiramis problem to a modern castle in Hungary—after that I never heard from him again.

The first Calderon act, ending with [Assyrian king] Ninus' marriage and with Menon's blinding, offers rich possibilities. The second act ends with the victory of Ninyas [Semiramis' son]. Third act: Semiramis as Ninyas, and her death. The third act is the most difficult; Hofmannsthal sensed this. Do you consider it possible to serve up an opera from Hofmannsthal's phantastic and profound fragment and Calderon's drama?

I would prefer that you did it by yourself. If it cannot be otherwise, together with Lernet H. How long will you stay in Vienna? What are your next addresses? Best wishes,

Dr. Richard Strauss

Garmisch
April 22, 1935

Dear Herr Zweig,

Herr Lernet-Holenia has had his two so-called comedies, *Alkestis* and *Die Frau des Potiphar*, sent to me, and after reading them with indignation, I frankly don't know what to think of you. You cannot seriously believe that a man capable of publishing such silly, tasteless, and witless stuff could write a libretto for me? I remember *Österreichische Komödie* as a somewhat thin but still rather nice comedy; *Die Standarte*, which I am now reading has great narrative merits, but the lyrical elements show serious weaknesses—it is hard to believe that the same man who wrote this relatively good book should sink so low as to write *Alkestis*.

Alfred Kerr once started a saucy operetta for me, after Wieland's *Peregrinus Proteus*.[48] This essay was pure Bernard Shaw compared with *Alkestis*. I showed it to Hofmannsthal; he was dismayed and furious. No, dear Herr Zweig, this will not do. If you desert me now, now that you have written your admirable libretto *Die schweigsame Frau*, I have no choice left but to retire. Let me soon hear from you. All best wishes, sincerely,

Dr. Richard Strauss

Garmisch
April 23, 1935

Dear Herr Zweig,

Calderon's *Semiramis* is the only other heroic theme I know that also has a romantic element. If you could get interested in giving it shape and if you believe that its plot and its main character could appeal to contemporary audiences, the subject could yield a spectacular opera and much opportunity for the musician.

It would make no difference to me, what format you use for it.

It may even be possible to make two operas out of it: first evening, the Menon tragedy as prelude in four to five scenes, two and a half hours, like *Rheingold*; second evening, the tragedy Semiramis-Lidor-Ninyas-Asträa, perhaps in three acts. Do you have the Hofmannsthal fragment? *La hija del aire* is included in translation as *Tochter der Luft* in the four-volume Calderon edition of the Deutsche Klassikerbibliothek, Leipzig, published by Hesse und Becker Verlag.

Goethe thought highly of the play. I would love to compose one more grand opera, with ballet, pageant march, battle music, and so on. The opera could start with a fight between the two goddesses Venus and Diana at the birth of Semiramis, and the two ladies could participate in the action later, too.

Excuse these suggestions. But from my work with Hofmannsthal I am used to saying everything that pops into my head. Perhaps such idle thought will catch fire some time in the mind of the recipient. Warm wishes, sincerely,

Dr. Richard Strauss

Where do you wish me to mail the promised manuscript of the piano score?

Garmisch
April 24, 1935

Dear Herr Zweig,

I keep turning Semiramis around in my head. I diligently worked through Calderon again, and then reread Hofmannsthal's visions, which contain much depth and greatness. Someone like Shakespeare could create a magnificent work from Calderon and Hofmannsthal. Would you like to be that Shakespeare? I can't do it. I could only write the music.

Let me comment on Calderon himself, and let me use plain language to make myself clear. The Menon tragedy is plain and unequivocal. I am now relying entirely on Hofmannsthal: The two husbands who fight for the woman; she herself decides for the more powerful and becomes queen: Cosima Wagner motive!

(In the second part of Calderon, the great courtesan is missing: Catherine II. Agrippina/Nero; in love with her own son Ninyas. Seduction of the enemy: Lidor.

The second part could begin with the love night with the captured enemy, then morning grooming—unkempt to war— Lidor's betrayal and punishment, and so on. Then love for the servant, Phryxus—as we have said: Venus is missing in Calderon. Actually the motive is a reversal of that in Schiller's *Jungfrau*.

Semiramis is strong as long as she loves, invincible; as merely Statesman Ninyas she is mortal: Diana's victory over Venus.)

Are these sketchy comments of any use to you?

I think there is enough fine material here for a Shakespeare, but I am not cut out for that.

I leave for Kissingen tomorrow (Dapper's sanatorium) and hope to get good news from you there. Please let me know your next addresses. With good wishes,

Dr. Richard Strauss

Hotel Regina, Vienna
April 26, 1935

My dear Herr Doctor,

I am writing to you today at great length, and I would count myself fortunate if I were able to advise you about your choice of texts at this decisive moment. You feel yourself, and I can fully appreciate it, that this is a historical moment in your career because your talent, now at its peak, surely must be exercised only for a decisive work. I was sorry that Lernet-Holenia did not appeal to you. He is a mysterious person as a poet, magnificent in his poems and in some of his dramatic scenes, then again incredibly negligent, when he writes comedies or light novels with his left hand and to earn money, and these lack depth and charm. I thought that working with you would stimulate his highest creativity because I feel that when his passion is aroused he is greater than all others.

In the next few days I will seriously look into *Semiramis*. Rossini already felt that it had the makings of an opera. I remember several impressive scenes and also the élan of the overture. I entirely understand why you find the material attractive: the impressive personality, the mighty passion, the heroic atmosphere, and the tropical colorfulness, so well suited to the intoxicating power of your music. When, on your suggestion, I exposed myself to this material, it elicited a strange association. I remembered another work, with a similar setting. Perhaps you know it, but you might order it for reading in any case: it is *Sardanapal* by Byron—I am sure you can get it in Kissingen in a good German translation. There is the same sybaritic atmosphere as in *La hija del aire* although the motif is quite different: the effeminate, gluttonous king, losing his realm as a result of his debauchery, allowing his enemies to close in, but waking up grandiosely at the last minute, and magnificently going down in the flames. At first sight, this theme seems quite different from that of *Semiramis*, but I wonder whether it might not be possible to transfer this stupendous ending to *Semiramis*, an ending akin to the finale in *Götterdämmerung*, a glorious cataclysm. In this way we might have that tragic third act that Calderon could not find and that Hofmannsthal looked for in vain: a demonic crash, which destroys everything carnal, and gloriously leads to the heroic. I hope I have expressed myself clearly. With your sure instinct you will sense that the usual theater finale with suicide, dagger, or poison would not be appropriate for this tragedy; now you will want to read the finale from *Sardanapal*, although born from a different atmosphere, and I believe it would provide a truly heroic solution that opens the greatest orchestral possibilities for music, especially your music. Besides, the intervention of the gods also will have to be changed, I feel. They should not be the classic, conventional Venus and Diana, but archaic godheads of that world of grand images, Asiatic godheads who are *not* familiar to us, and who would provide a novel effect by their strangeness and unfamiliar symbolism.

This is the way in which I see in outline (you will soon hear more from me) the potentials of such a "spectacular opera" as you correctly designated it, an opera to which, for highest perfection and effect, the heroic element would have to be added to the erotic, and the mythical element to the sensuous. The opera would have to have something of the magic bounty of *Die aegyptische Helena* without its darkness; a mania derived not only from vulgar sensuousness but from the spiritual and heroic.

Now to practical things. Unhappily I am denied the free and natural ways to offer you my help and my full working capacity. I believe you know and value Joseph Gregor.[49] I feel he is the greatest theater expert. He has just completed some outstanding poetical adaptations of classic Spanish plays, above all Calderon's *El Principe Constante* [*The Constant Prince*] to be played at the Burgtheater, and the *Cenodoxus** adaptation, equally an outstanding poetical accomplishment. There is hardly anyone who excels him in dramaturgic expertise. (You know his *Weltgeschichte des Theaters*; an equally eminent book about Shake-

---

* *Cenodoxus, Doktor von Paris*, a German baroque drama by Jakob Bidermann (1578–1639), after the legend of Saint Bruno of Cologne, with motifs from *Faust, Everyman*, and the story of the Prodigal Son.

speare is about to be published.) Joseph Gregor is one of my *intimate friends*; with him I could discuss in detail the plan and execution of each scene; I would never boast having counseled this old and trusted friend in his work. He is unassailable as a person, measured with the strict yardstick of present-day requirements. I believe that in this arrangement he could be your best collaborator, and you would know that I, bound to him in friendship and to you in admiration, would participate in his work with true devotion. With your permission, I shall discuss the Semiramis plan with him in detail; in the meantime, you might study the last act of *Sardanapal* to see whether the final heroic cataclysm of self-destruction would seem the appropriate culmination of such a work.

After I have talked with him and worked the plans through with him, I shall write to you. I also hope that meanwhile you will have received my book about Maria Stuart that has just started its way into this world. If you are planning to give me the pleasure of sending me that piano manuscript of *Die schweigsame Frau*, please mail it to Herbert Reichner Verlag, Vienna, Millergasse 39, who will keep it for me. I will stay here only till May 6 and then go away for a few weeks, probably to Italy. Devotedly,

Stefan Zweig

P.S.   Joseph Gregor would, of course, see you at once as soon as the scenario plans are clear, to discuss everything with you.

Bad Kissingen
April 29, 1935

Dear Herr Zweig,

I am moved by your modesty and your kind willingness to help; let me sincerely thank you. If you think you can work with that splendid man Gregor, I am of course in full agreement. I am intensely interested in your thoughts about Semiramis. I will read *Sardanapal* at once, and am impatiently waiting for further news from you. I am extraordinarily attracted by that figure.

Fürstner will mail the manuscripts to the indicated Vienna
address right away. With warm wishes, your highly excited,
grateful

Dr. Richard Strauss

Bad Kissingen
May 1, 1935

Dear Herr Zweig,

I finished reading Byron's *Sardanapal*. Poetically the main
figure is superb but entirely undemonic. The end is beautiful,
but, unfortunately, already adapted by Richard Wagner for his
Ring. Can it be used a second time? I am waiting for your further
news. I'll stay in Garmisch until May 20. On June 1, I will conduct *Feuersnot* in Munich. On June 5, *Arabella*, and on June 11,
Frau ohne Schatten, a new production by [conductor Hans]
Knappertsbusch. Could we meet one of these days? In Munich or
Salzburg? Sincerely,

Dr. Richard Strauss

Hotel Regina, Vienna
May 3, 1935

My dear Herr Doctor,

This is only an interim letter. I shall write to you in more
detail tomorrow about my long conference with Joseph Gregor
about Semiramis, which have led to a basic dramatic outline.
As for myself, I cannot quite overcome my fear that Semiramis will
arouse negative feelings in the audience. In the drama, and even
more so in music, the listener is moved by a character expressing
pure feelings, not by a hating, violent, demonic figure; even
Electra would be intolerable as a musical figure if (in the scene
with her sister and when recognizing Orestes) her bitterness did
not find that beautiful lyrical and feminine solution. I discussed
with Gregor a similar break in the domineering, destructive,
demonic temperament of Semiramis; I will explain our suggestion

for a solution in my detailed letter tomorrow. I am wondering whether the predominating force of Semiramis does not reside in her superhuman rather than her human nature—well, I'll talk about this tomorrow.

Another plan in which we see an opportunity for a colorful opera would be the world of Mexico—in very distant similarity to Gerhart Hauptmann's *Der weisse Heiland*. You may be familiar with the legend, according to which before Cortez, that is before the brutal conquerors, another European, a legendary figure, arrived in Mexico. He was revered there as a saint, but finally cruelly murdered by the priests. It would be thrilling to revive the lost wonder world of the Aztecs with their dances, festivals, war expeditions, and songs, and to juxtapose the cruel, barbarian sacrifices with the lyrical figure of that stranger who will be slaughtered (in connection with female episodes); and as a finale, in revenge, the invasion of the Spaniards, the lightning destruction of this barbarian-aristocratic world. Perhaps you know Eduard Stucken's novel *Die weissen Götter*, in which that orgiastic atmosphere is described. This theme would provide the basis for a spectacular opera (quite different from Gasparo Spontini's dry opera *Fernand Cortes*) and at the same time show the religious ethical conflict between the pure (in a high sense Christian) stranger and those demonic-fascinating civilizations. I note this plan in the margin, as it were; perhaps you feel inclined to read Hauptmann's (dramatically weak) *Der weisse Heiland* or Stucken's outstanding *Die weissen Götter*—they make stimulating reading. I could imagine that you would find the strange, pungent scent of that world even more attractive than that of *Semiramis*. Tomorrow you will hear from me about my as yet only summarized structure for *Semiramis*, which, of course, would have to be raised far beyond the Calderon plot. Meanwhile just hasty greetings, tomorrow my full letter. Respectfully,

Stefan Zweig

Joseph Gregor is already enthusiastically preparing the scenario.[50]

Bad Kissengen
May 4, 1935

Dear Herr Zweig,

Gregor wrote me a very cordial letter.[51] I am most anxious to learn what you two have cooked up. I am not so sure about Gregor as I am about my proved and tested Zweig, and am therefore asking, first, for your active participation in *Semiramis* and, second, that you not abandon our two previous ideas: *1648* and *Dopo la musica*; nor *Celestina*, which would interest me very much if you could succeed in creating a good, complete tragicomic comedy, to supplement the romantic pair and the magnificent woman matchmaker.

To make sure, in case *Semiramis* did not work out: do you and Gregor know Hofmansthal's drafts for *Semiramis*? With hope and thanks, sincerely,

Dr. Richard Strauss

I find your *Maria Stuart* very interesting; extraordinary how Schiller's ingenious instinct picked up the essential of this theme.

Hotel Regina, Vienna
May 4, 1935

My dear Herr Doctor,

I will try to summarize, after an exhaustive conference with Gregor, how he visualizes the dramatic plan for *Semiramis*. If the basic outline appeals to you, he would then work out the scenario and send it to you or see you personally.

The difficulty about the main figure is, of course, the demonic element, that is to say the nonhuman element, but since it is exactly that element that attracts you most, every effort must be made to stress this mystic and nonhuman facet.

According to our conference, Gregor is thinking of a prelude with some godheads who warn the guard (called by Calderon, too classically, Tiresias) about the disaster that will happen if this

woman demon is set free to roam the world of mortals. Semiramis
is not seen at first, and can only be heard from her prison, which
would not be a cave, as Calderon has it, but a sort of Assyrian
temple. The guard succumbs to her persuasive voice and, forgetting
his duty, leaves for a while. Meanwhile (in accordance with
Calderon) Menon comes along hunting, hears the wailing voice,
and is moved. He rejects all warnings—those from the guard who
comes rushing back and those from the mysterious bird choirs
(to be taken over from Calderon); he forces his way in and sets her
free. The choirs keep warning, the desperate guard commits
suicide by throwing himself down an abyss.

I consider this a grand mythical prelude, but every effort would
have to be made to avoid any reminder of the Brunhilde liberation;
it would be a forceful opening and would show the link between
Semiramis and the superhuman element.

The first act would then be a variant of the Gyges-Kandaules
motif, showing that Menon cannot keep his tongue. At a
feast he praises the beauty of the mysterious woman, whom
he has so far not shown to anyone; he allows himself to be
lured into presenting her to the king. The king instantly
succumbs to her magic. He wants to buy her, and Semiramis
immediately goes over to him. The episode ends, as with Calderon,
with the blinding of Menon and the elevating of Semiramis, who
becomes queen. (Here perhaps a female opposite figure might be
introduced, a tender, lyrical queen who is repudiated; she would
constitute a human female foil for the demonic Semiramis.)
Menon, after his blinding, would not be lost to the tragedy, but
would, as a blind man, like a slave throughout the play grope
around after the queen who had him blinded—a grandiose touch.
This blind man would exemplify more than anybody else the
woman's demonism.

The second act would bring a further heightening of the story.
Semiramis wrings the power from the king's hands, subjugates
everybody to her will, and creates terrible crises. Finally she uses
the infatuation of the king's brother (or somebody else's) to free
herself from the king. He is murdered by conspirators, but now,

instead of rewarding the conspirators, she has them also murdered or imprisoned. She wants all power for herself. Now that she has it, at the palace and in the state, she calls upon the people to go to war against other nations so that she can dominate the earth and become the queen of the world. The act ends with a call to arms to the whole nation. This end seems to me to offer the grand heroic finale you need.

The third act, whose problem Hofmannsthal recognized, would have to elevate the tragic into the grandiose, by further increasing Semiramis' hybris. She returns home in triumph, she has conquered all nations, the kings of the world woo her. She rejects them all, her ambition rises higher yet—she wants to be mistress not only of the earth but also of the heavens. She orders all statues of the gods destroyed. These statues in stone or bronze would represent the same godheads who appeared on the stage at the prelude of the opera. Again warning birds' choirs and other demonic symbols are heard or seen, but she is not deterred from her decision and the statues of the godheads are tumbled. Only a last, closed shrine is left and should serve, as in the Calderon original, to paraphrase Semiramis' love-hate toward her son Ninyas. To enslave her, the gods create a kind of male mirror-image of her. At the moment when this last shrine is torn open, she steps out of it herself in a male mirror-image. And this woman, who up to now has rejected all, is transported into ecstasy, woos that alter ego. This demonstrates also visually that her own capacity to love is an enormous, demonic self-love. But the demonic mirror-image recedes when she approaches it, wards her off as she pursues it, and vanishes entirely. At this point, mockingly and sneeringly, the birds' choir could set in and introduce her downfall. Now that she has become weak, all rebel against her, and an end similar to that of Sardanapal would have to follow—she locks herself in and in a frenzy destroys herself.

This would be the basic draft as Gregor wants to work it out. You will hear further details from him. I have already indicated my objections, in principle, against that figure which is so dear to you. I have always considered the audience's sympathy with a stage figure the secret of theatrical success; I doubt whether it will be possible to create real admiration for Semiramis or even real compassion for her when she destroys herself. But since the figure fascinates you so much, Gregor would like to work out a scenario and further complement it in a discussion with you.

My regards for Mrs. Strauss and my respect for you, sincerely,

Stefan Zweig

Permanent address: care of Herbert Reichner Verlag, Vienna, VI, Millergasse 39.

Bad Kissingen
May 5, 1935

Dear Herr Zweig,

Thank you so much for your Mexican letter, which I received this morning. I will be glad to read Stucken and Hauptmann. Perhaps you are not aware how passionate an anti-Christ I am, and that the red Savior will be as obnoxious to me as the white one will probably be uninteresting. In *Salome* I tried to compose the good Jochanaan more or less as a clown; a preacher in the desert, especially one who feeds on grasshoppers, seems infinitely comical to me. Only because I have already caricatured the five Jews and also poked fun at Father Herodes did I feel that I had to follow the law of contrast and write a pedantic-Philistine motif for four horns to characterize Jochanaan.

No—such a passive prophet battling the ol' high priests, and at the end the awful Cortez: I don't think that's my dish. And the good Aztecs are not in my backyard either. If I have to choose, I'd rather take that monster Semiramis, who has at least some air of grandeur as a general and ruler. I do not always need to compose the Sweet Viennese Girl. Perhaps that Assyrian woman could be assigned some features of your Maria Stuart in that Semiramis is invincible as long as she dominates men in every respect until the moment that she succumbs to a Bothwell. Or is such "slave love" incompatible with the idea of Semiramis?

For the time being, then, I'll stick to my request in my letter yesterday: Celestine or Semiramis.† Sincerely,

Dr. Richard Strauss

† Prince or rascal, but no paragons of virtue and martyrs.

[Zurich, May 9, 1935 (postmark)]
Hotel Bellerive, Utoquai

[Postal card]
My dear Herr Doctor,
   In a few days you will receive a detailed draft from Professor Gregor; [52] I will also write soon. I will be busy here at the library for two or three weeks. Devotedly,

Stefan Zweig

Bad Kissingen
May 12, 1935

Dear Herr Zweig,
   Good old Gregor writes enthusiastically, but enthusiasm alone won't do it. I will be glad to wait and examine what he offers, but to get a Semiramis that is better than even Calderon's I really would need a Shakespeare, and for now Gregor would have to prove that he is at least a Kotzebue, let alone a Scribe. *Vederemo.* At any rate, please don't set aside *your* drafts for me. I need a poet! Devotedly,

Dr. Richard Strauss

Bad Kissingen
May 17, 1935

Dear Herr Zweig,
   You must have read Gregor's fetus by now.[53] Any critique is superfluous. A philologist's childish fairytale. If *you* are not able

to forge a "grand opera" for me from Calderon's work, I'll just have
to forget it. But how am I to tell dear Gregor?

Now what? Please don't *you* forsake me!

To Garmisch on Monday! Sincerely, your desperate

Dr. Richard Strauss

Once and for all, please stop urging new poets upon me.

Hotel Bellerive [Zurich]
Utoquai
May 19, 1935

My dear Herr Doctor,

I also received Gregor's draft and wrote to him at once that I
don't consider it viable in that form. What succeeded in the
Ring to some extent—letting the gods intervene in human affairs—
here seems impossible because these gods are concepts rather than
personifications, they are not persons that can be put on the stage.

Semiramis, what problems! Hofmannsthal sensed, I believe, the
resistance that her blood-thirsty strangeness provokes, and his
instinct was correct. *Sympathy*, the basis of all effectiveness on
the stage, will never be elicited by this superwoman. Besides, the
link with the present time is lacking, whereas Wagner in his
Ring wanted to create a Germanic mythology and, also, with the
gold, curse the contemporary ideology of capitalism. Semiramis
remains a priestly figure, spiritually unrelated to our time. I
expressed these doubts from the outset.

I would like to remind you of Kleist's *Amphitryon*, a comedy
with depth, an eternal problem, combining coarse-comical and
sublime elements, a bewitching female figure, and, despite Molière,
a German work. How beautifully the music could distinguish the
false Amphitryon from the real one; what is hardly distinguish-
able in the comedy could be differentiated by music. There would
also be a chance for the spectacular, the martial departure, and

the religious spirit. A Greek comedy has never been set to music, and the material, if skillfully shaped, would suit you well, I believe. And the announcement of Heracles, the vanishing of the gods— what a finale! It's all there, and the basic tone would be, if I may say so, one of wise and profound cheerfulness. I never could understand why no German composer ever reached for this and why Hugo Wolf dreamed about Penthesilea, that other Semiramis.

What a pity that I cannot work for you freely and openly. But the official measures, instead of becoming milder or more conciliatory, have only grown harsher. Some of these measures cannot but offend one's sense of honor; what one sincerely hoped and felt obliged to hope proved to be erroneous. You will discover yourself, I fear, that the cultural development will more and more go to the side of the extremists. Let us hope that at least *Die schweigsame Frau*, out of consideration for you, will pass without needless argument, but it represents a unique and nonrepeatable exception in the present situation, and there is no indication of a reversal of the trend. You are also aware that it was not up to me, and you are also aware of my cordial friendship with the men of Insel Verlag; and yet, with a wounded heart, I have to leave this haven of thirty years' standing, no matter how much we both had wished it otherwise. As an individual one cannot resist the will or insanity of a whole world; enough strength is needed to remain firm and self-respecting and to reject all feelings of bitterness and hatred. This alone has become a sort of accomplishment these days, and is almost harder than writing books.

Whenever I should be in a position to counsel one of your collaborators, though, I will gladly volunteer. It must not be, as Schiller says, that "such geniuses rest." Who should create great music in our time, if your hand pauses!

As ever, respectfully,

Stefan Zweig

Garmisch
May 21, 1935

Dear Herr Zweig,

Your letter is very painful for me. I can understand that you have misgivings. But your misgivings cannot be greater than mine. Neither of us can follow a path different from that prescribed by our artistic conscience. Only one command exists for us; to be creative for the good of mankind.

Whether and when our creation will be shown on the stage is something we must not think about today.

Amphitryon is not to my taste at all. The material is still colder and more unappealing than the story of Semiramis, which, at least, is spectacular.

I now must see you personally. Could I meet with you this week somewhere? In Landeck or Bregenz? If it cannot be helped I will come to meet you in Zurich. But I would prefer a suitable place in the middle.[54] On May 28 and 29 I will be in Munich—I take it that you cannot go there or to Lindau, can you?

Please answer by telegram. With good wishes, sincerely

Dr. Richard Strauss

Garmisch
May 22, 1935

Dear Herr Zweig,

Yesterday, for your sake, I reread Kleist's *Amphitryon*. I saw it performed last year in the Munich Residenz Theater before a totally apathetic audience and I am respectfully surprised that you recommend that an opera be produced from this cold, unattractive play. The best thing about it is the sophisticated dialogue, most of which would have to be cut or be only half understood if sung. The great scene in which Jupiter reveals himself to Alkmene is artificial brainwork that sounds like the pleading of a Jewish lawyer. Believe me: Kleist is beyond composing. I just saw it again when [the German composer Paul] Graener cut down the opera

Der Prinz von Homburg to a few claptrap scenes, even provided some decent music: the box-office result, despite Prussian flags and real military bands, was 700 marks from the patriotic Berlin audience at the third showing.

Could we meet during the next few days?

Semiramis at least is a splendid opera figure.

Good wishes, sincerely,

Dr. Richard Strauss

Garmisch
May 24, 1935

Dear Herr Zweig,

Yesterday I was surprised by a visit from [the Austrian composer and conductor Emil Nikolaus Freiherr von] Rezniček, who is a houseguest and will stay till Monday morning. On Tuesday I have to go to Munich where I am tied up till June 11 with conducting and assisting with rehearsals for *Die Frau ohne Schatten*. On June 12 I am going to Dresden, hence won't be able to see you before June 29. I have to assume that you won't be able to come to Dresden. This is a great pity! How long will you stay in Zurich? And where will you go afterward? After I am through with Dresden I must see you. Until then, please give my artistic needs some thought. You are the only one who can carve the grand opera *Semiramis* for me from Calderon's material. The first half, until Menon's blinding, is fairly self-evident, perhaps with a prelude, in which the stories of Tiresias and of Semiramis' birth visibly take place in a dramatic scene between the two antagonistic goddesses. The scene in which Ninus wants to persuade Menon to forego Semiramis is utterly magnificent. The lesser scenes, on the other hand, especially the garden scene with the listening Ninus, are old-fashioned theater. More difficult is the problem with Semiramis as Ninus' murderer, as a ruler, and as a mother. But precisely about the tragedy Semiramis-Ninyas your suggestions were so ingenious (also the Sardanapal finale seems plausible to me) that I have the distinct impression your expertise could fashion an opera for me from that material if you only seriously wanted to. For this job I can't use an enthusiastic philologist; I need a real poet and a creative theater expert. Please, immerse yourself seriously in this challenge—you will even turn Semiramis into an appealing figure for me, just as you succeeded with the obnoxious Morosus.

I also consider Celestine possible, if fashioned by your hand; and, likewise, I would welcome any material created by *yourself*.

But don't you recommend any other librettist to me. Nothing comes of it, it isn't worth the paper.

Again, please send me your next addresses, good wishes, your sincerely,

Dr. Richard Strauss

Garmisch
May 25, 1935

Dear Herr Zweig,

Fürstner sent me the proofs of the libretto. If you approve, I'd decide on "Freely adapted from Ben Jonson."[55] The slip of the pen, reading "Timidia" in the second act, and later, when she is in a frenzy, familiarly addressed by him as "Timida," I considered a joke. Couldn't we leave it that way now that the score has been printed?[56] I told Fürstner that a few lines not composed by me will be in the libretto nevertheless. "Mit Reverenz" I have included in the composition, also "Monteverdi." If you want "Orkan" with Morosus, we can put it in the printed libretto. I composed "Ocean." What about *contractus matrimoniae*? †

I have informed Fürstner in the sense discussed above. If you do not agree, please let him know. Good wishes,

Dr. Richard Strauss

[In the margin]: † Could we let this stand as a joke? The comedians' Latin is not perfcet.

Garmisch
May 27, 1935

Dear Herr Zweig,

I expect to be in Munich on Saturday (Hotel Vierjahreszeiten) and could be in Bregenz (Hotel Montfort) on Sunday, June 2, noon. Please wire whether you will be able to see me there. Sincerely,

Dr. Richard Strauss

Hotel Bellerive, Zurich
June 3, 1935

Dear Herr Doctor,

I telephoned Joseph Gregor this morning. He'll come here Sunday and will then start working according to my instructions, and I will work with him in line with your intentions.

I am on friendly terms with one of the major literary agents. If you really plan to finish your biographical recollections, he would like to approach you for *world* rights. It would be a mistake to give such a manuscript to *one* publisher. A general agent can obtain enormous fees for prepublication rights and the rights for all languages in the world; I am sure you could get an advance of $20,000, which, after all, is money and represents only the *minimum*.† I would be glad to send you that man. As fill-in work, this autobiography would not only be refreshing for you but also rewarding provided it is handled in this way. But soon you'll be ready for the real work!

Respectfully,

Stefan Zweig

† The royalties may easily be a multiple of that.

Garmisch
June 8, 1935

Dear Herr Zweig,

Thank you so much for your kind hint; but I am not thinking of publishing my personal notes during my lifetime.[57] Besides, it bores me to prepare the work in final form. I just sketch what is important, provide some signposts, and then leave it to the scholars to fill in. I write things helter-skelter and without organization as they pop into my head. Beyond that, and with renewed thanks for the enjoyable day in Bregenz, I am patiently waiting. I very much liked *1648* after your oral presentation. Also the two one-act plays.

Give my regards to dear Gregor, but as for libretti I prefer to sit on *one*—asset.

Will be in Dresden (Hotel Bellevue) on Wednesday and will report to you about the rehearsals. With good wishes,

Dr. Richard Strauss

June 9, 1935

Dear Herr Zweig,

I know friend Gregor is with you. In his highly interesting *Shakespeare* I find on page 363 the ingenious reason why the poet in *Henry IV* introduced the magnificent Falstaff. As in our *Semiramis*, an appealing figure was missing. Hence your idea of assigning this role to a wife of Ninus. This Falstaff gives me the idea that in *Semiramis* the comic figures of Chato and the siren (or similar balancing figures) may be necessary. It's just an idea. I'll be in Dresden after Wednesday.

Regards to you both, your

Dr. Richard Strauss

[Enclosure: Schedule of the Dresden rehearsals of *Die schweigsame Frau*.]

Dresden
June 13, 1935

Dear Herr Zweig,

Just got your letter. Your collaboration with good Gregor makes my skin crawl. Why do you insist *à tout prix* on saddling me with an erudite philologist? My librettist is Zweig; he needs no collaborators—as you could have convinced yourself yesterday after the rehearsal of the first act. Your libretto is simply first rate, the act finales terrific. Things go so well that only the finest points of the dialogue need more work. Gielen and Bohm are equally excellent. Cebotari charming, just made for that part.[58] You can rest assured: that opera is a bull's-eye, even if it has to wait until the twenty-first century. But don't bother me with the old Mexicans. You write those two operas for me, as you told them to me in Bregenz: *1648* (it was superb)! and the comic opera *Prima la musica* (in Eichendorff's style, for all I care)—that's all I need. The Silent One will be on the radio on July 8, unabridged. Here the rumor is making the rounds that you have assigned your royalties to the Jewish Emergency Fund. I have denied it.

Hurriedly,

Dr. Richard Strauss

June 17, 1935[59]

Dear Herr Zweig,*

Your letter of the 15th** is driving me to distraction! This Jewish obstinacy! Enough to make an anti-Semite of a man! This pride of race, this feeling of solidarity! Do you believe that I am ever, in any of my actions, guided by the thought that I am "German" (perhaps, *qui le sait*)? Do you believe that Mozart composed as an "Aryan"? I know only two types of people: those with and those without talent. The people exist for me only at the moment they become audience. Whether they are Chinese, Bavarians, New Zealanders, or Berliners leave me cold. What mat-

---

* This letter was intercepted by the Gestapo and never reached Zweig. See note 59.
** See Foreword, p. xxiii.

ters is that they pay full price for admission. Now please stop
plagueing me with that good Gregor. The comedy you sent me[60]
is charming and I don't doubt one moment that it is your idea
exclusively. I won't accept it under an assumed name, no more
than *1648*. So I urgently ask you again to work out those two one-act
plays as soon as possible; name your terms. Just keep the matter
a secret on *your* part and let *me* worry about what I will do with
the plays. Who told you that I have exposed myself politically?
Because I have conducted a concert in place of Bruno Walter? That
I did for the orchestra's sake. Because I substituted for Toscanini?
That I did for the sake of Bayreuth. That has nothing to do with
politics. It is none of my business how the boulevard press
interprets what I do, and it should not concern you either. Because
I ape the president of the Reich Music Chamber? That I do only
for good purposes and to prevent greater disasters! I would have
accepted this troublesome honorary office under any government,
but neither Kaiser Wilhelm nor Herr Rathenau offered it to
me. So be a good boy, forget Moses and the other apostles for a
few weeks, and work on *your* two one-act plays. Maybe the
Mexican text could become a good opera, but not for me. I am
not interested in Indians, red or white gods, and Spanish conflicts
of conscience. Let Gregor finish that text, but for another composer who surely will be more appreciative than your well-
wishing equally stubborn

Dr. Richard Strauss

Regards for the well-being of your mother. The show here will
be terrific. Everybody is wildly enthusiastic. And with all this you
ask me to forego you? Never ever!

June 22, 1935

Dear Herr Zweig,
    I hope you are not too angry about my last letter. I am still so
desperate about your obstinacy of wanting to foist on me your
own work under someone else's name.

If you just could see and hear *how* good our work is, you would drop all race worries and political misgivings with which you, incomprehensibly to me, unnecessarily weigh down your artist's mind, and you would write as much as possible for me and not have anything written by others. Let me worry about the rest. I have enough grief already, don't add to my sorrow.[61] The performance here will be highly satisfying. Sixty-one-year-old Plaschke is *the* Morosus, just needs to play himself; Cebotari is a miracle of energy, theatrical talent, and charm, such as are hard to find these days; also Aminta. The others, magnificently directed by Gielen, are fabulous, sparkling with wit and buffoonery; the orchestra under Böhm, of course, splendid. Decorations and Fanto's costumes[62] are something to see and will be a sensation in London. The whole Dresden ensemble is slated to give a guest performance there. Dr. Goebbels, who will be here with his wife on Monday, will give a government subsidy for this.[63] As you see, the nasty Third Reich has its good aspects, too. Besides, Minister of War Blomberg and seven foreign officers are expected. There is still silence about Hitler's attending. At any rate, the opera is magnificent, truly an entirely perfect, mature masterpiece; it would be a pity if I were to scuttle composing now.

With best wishes and grateful congratulations, loyally,

Dr. Richard Strauss

Garmisch
June 28, 1935

Dear Herr Zweig,

Back last night at 12:30 A.M., returning from Dresden by car. (The second showing despite tropical heat, not a subscription performance, astonishingly well attended; this time the second act was better received than the first; very successful.) I intended to write to you anyway, and now can answer your cherished letter at the same time.[64] My, what odd ideas you have! Why should I become popular at any price, that is, tied to the rabble and per-

formed in every low-class theater? For a year I've tried hard at the
Propaganda Ministry to put an end to all those flea-bitten opera
joints that massacre *Lohengrin* with an orchestra of thirty
and a choir of fifteen; now finally I believe I have found an ally in
State Commissioner Hinkel who, together with Bruno von
Nissen,* may help me to persuade Dr. Goebbels to carry out my
long-cherished reform ideas to raise the quality of German
operatic culture.

This does not mean, however, that great and profound works of
art are to be cut down to the requirements of every clown that
runs a two-bit provincial stage—this I leave to Lehar and Puccini.
I'm thinking of true places of culture, medium-sized and large
opera houses that are to be enabled to present the masterpieces of
our German opera literature in the manner the composer desires.
This is to be done through increased grants which are to be tied
to definite standards of the repertory and production guidelines of
the highest artistic quality, through larger orchestras, expanded
ensembles, increased budgets for sets, and so on.

For this reason, an adaptation for normal theaters, as you
propose, is out of the question. Outside of difficulties in singing
and acting, the *Schweigsame* makes no extraordinary demands.

Arabella: a normal orchestra and one set! How much less do you
want? I don't compose for provincial stages with orchestras of
fewer than fifty players or for traveling shows.

The *Salome* premiere in Dresden had an orchestra of 105, and
all the world pessimistically predicted: well, two or three theaters
will perform that, and that's all. And in how many places has
this opera been shown! Thank heavens, I did not have to listen
to any of these adaptations for a reduced orchestra, although they
were possible in this instance. The difficulties of the *Schweigsame*
cannot be reduced below my own directives. Let them work hard,
and those who are too lazy had better keep their hands off and

* Hans Hinkel, secretary-general of the Reich "Chamber of Music"; Bruno
von Nissen, stage director and intendant, Strauss's colleague in the Nazi
Reich Chamber.

play operettas. I have never had the talent to write what can be performed easily; that is the special gift of inferior musicians. But now, once and for all: please, please, work for me on the two plays that you alone thought up: *1648* and the comedy *Prima la musica*, but without Gregor whose collaboration I strictly refuse; I don't compose camouflaged operas.

If good old Gregor will send me an independent new creation (up to now he has not been able to elicit my confidence) or if he, together with you, produces *Semiramis* or something entirely new, I will sympathetically consider everything—but texts invented by Zweig I will compose only under the name of Zweig.

What happens thereafter let be my worry, please.

Little Cebotari at Dresden was simply a dream come true. If such an interpreter for such an exceptional part could be found for the world premiere, one need not worry about the future. (How long did I have to wait with *Salome*—and am still waiting!)

"Get going, then, forward!" [65] I'm waiting!

With good wishes, your grateful and loyal

Dr. Richard Strauss

Garmisch
June 29, 1935

Dear Herr Zweig,

As I think over the experiences of the past few weeks I conclude that now, after *Arabella* and *Die schweigsame Frau*, only a serious subject would be appropriate. Your comedy draft is charming (although, a small weakness, there are too few purely lyrical scenes, that is, too many are laced with farcical passages); but it is in some respects reminiscent of *Ariadne*, and I need now an entirely different subject matter to remain creative. The more I think about *1648* the more I like the theme, and so I ask you urgently to work it out for me soonest (but without Gregor and under your own name and your own responsibility).

I asked dear old Gregor today to visit me here; [66] I hope I will

be able, then, to clarify in an honest exchange our relationship
and the question of future collaboration.

With good wishes, your

Dr. Richard Strauss

Garmisch
October 31, 1935

Dear Herr Doctor,

Thank you so much for your efforts concerning *Friedenstag*.
Your version is better fitted for the stage and more concise than
that of our friend Gr. But I cannot give my decision yet, because
the ending does not yet have the shape I requested from the
author. For several weeks I have been busy composing, but I have
not found the music that I expect of myself. The whole subject
is, after all, a bit too commonplace—soldiers, war, famine, medieval
heroism, dying together—it isn't quite my dish, with the best of
good will. Our good friend doubtless is very gifted—but he lacks
the higher creative power and ideas that stray a bit from the
widely traveled path. His sharp instincts for the stage are also
a dubious blessing. This is particularly noticeable in his *Daphne*,
whose appealing basic idea is not worked out at all. Lots of
words, schoolmarm banalities, no concentration on one focus; no
gripping human conflict.

Daphne (very pale), Apollo, and Leukippos would have to
clash in a Kleistian scene;[67] Daphne, rather than staying a dull
virgin, would have to love them both, the god and the human.
Zeus-Wotan preaching great wisdoms is just impossible; the
Medusa pantomime on the stage will provoke ridicule at best—no
audience in the world will be interested in this material, appealing as it is, in this form. Gr., infatuated by his own verse without
being his own audience, is lacking the ultimate, the decisive.
Wouldn't you yourself work on something for me? *Celestine*, and
Poi le parole, doppo la musica? I read a lot about de Casti in da
Ponte's memoirs.

For the last years of my life I would like to get some pleasure

out of my work, even if I have to put it away in my desk quietly.
I wrote this to you before. My literary estate! *Friedenstag* is too
labored—Gr.'s verses have no depth and are just superficially
pleasant without music.

I am mailing this letter from Tyrol and am asking that you had
also better not write to me across the German border because
all mail is being opened. Please sign your name as Henry Mor;
I will sign as Robert Storch.* It would be best if you were to send
me mail by messenger or through Gregor.

With best wishes, sincerely,

Dr. Richard Strauss

As for the enclosed comedy: apart from a few coarse vulgarities,
I find the draft excellent, but I will never believe that Gregor
did it. You talked yourself about de Casti's play a year ago, also
about *1648*. You are kind and self-effacing in yielding your
authorship to good old Gr., and you are considerate toward me,
but I simply won't believe it and Gr. does not have what it takes
for a suitable libretto. So I am asking you again, do the play
yourself, and also *Celestine* if possible, which could make a very
merry affair if done by the right person. The character itself is
delicious and the lyric elements superb. I promise profound
discretion.

I expect to be in Antwerp and Paris in the second half of March.
Perhaps I could meet you there.

* "Strauss used the fictitious name of Robert Storch in his opera *Intermezzo*,
where he portrayed himself in the figure of Storch" (Robert Breuer, *Musical
America*, February, 1958).

Address for the next four weeks:
c/o Miss Lotte Altmann
Hotel Westminster
[December 1935]

Dear Herr Doctor,

I wired you while I was en route. I would never want to cause
you any inconvenience,[68] but I must confess that in this case I

wished to annoy the other gentleman, by inquiring, in passing, why I as a Viennese and Austrian was never informed about that matter. I knew very well that W. is no longer *persona grata*, and the serious error was *much* regretted—I immediately got some long, personal, and most pleasing information from Dr. Kerber.[69] I explicitly declared (I'll send you a copy of the letter) that I was not authorized and didn't have any right to negotiate but that as an Austrian and Viennese, in view of the supposed support for Austrian writers, I knew why nothing had happened so far. I know how painful it is for Herr W. (whom I detest) to also be asked about this matter by private persons, how much he'd like to hide behind an order from higher up, *which, however, does not exist.* You wouldn't believe how ridiculous the man made himself by constantly telephoning all editorial offices, by giving readings of his "poetic" works; to get rid of him soon is the unanimous wish of all to whom opera still means something. Nothing annoys him more than the creations and accomplishments of others. Your opera bothers him and he gets nervous when somebody mentions it. Well, it seems a worthy task, then, to make him a little more nervous yet.

I never considered the Volksoper.* But it is all to the good that Vienna is reminded of the existence of the work. The newspapers, except a minor one, have suppressed (perhaps following W.'s hint) any reporting of the intimate performance by the R. S. community;[70] They will suppress any mention of the Scala if they can. I think one should not make it too easy for the gentleman to give vent to his personal malices against a masterpiece. Hence, I, as a Viennese, made a very personal, nosy inquiry, stressing however, that I am asking only *ad personam.* You will receive a carbon copy tomorrow. Please trust the discretion of your devoted

Morosus

* Vienna's second opera house.

Appendix

"The History of Die schweigsame Frau"—*the heading is the author's own—is part of the writings found in the Richard Strauss estate and written in ordinary notebooks with blue or gray covers. The following essay is found in Number V of the blue notebooks.*

The History of *Die schweigsame Frau*
By Richard Strauss

Hugo von Hofmannsthal, attacked and maligned by the press and the profession for thirty years, is dead. He was a faithful genius, and I obstinately stuck with him. Now, after his premature death, he is finally recognized as "my true poet." I must resign myself to admitting that my period of creating operas has come to a close. *Salome* by Oscar Wilde, which the Viennese lyric poet Anton Lindner recognized as a covert opera text, was an exception. Hofmannsthal alone was the writer who, in addition to his poetic creativeness and his theatrical talent, had the sensitivity to offer a composer theater themes in a form suitable for composition. He was able to write a libretto that was at once effective on the stage, met high literary standards, and could be set to music. I flirted and negotiated with the best German poets, repeatedly with Gerhart Hauptmann; also with d'Annunzio. But in fifty years I found only the wonderful Hofmannsthal. He was resourceful in inventing musical themes. Although hardly "musical," he, like Goethe, had clear-sighted musical intuitions, and an astonishing flair for what subjects were germane for my requirements.

After *Intermezzo*, where I copied, as it were, with some dramaturgical finesse two tragicomic episodes of my family life and poured some music over the product, my "poetical potency" was definitely exhausted. When I had just about given up hope of ever finding a librettist again, I was visited by Anton Kippenberg of Insel-Verlag, who was on his way to Stefan Zweig in Salzburg. Earlier, in Vienna, I had seen Ben Jonson's *Volpone* and the amusing comedy *Das Lamm des Armen*. Casually I said to Kippenberg: Why don't you ask Zweig (whom I did not know in person) whether he has an opera subject for me. That was in the winter 1931–1932. Presently I got a letter from Zweig, saying he did in fact have some thoughts but until now had not been bold enough to present them to me. We made an appointment in Munich, where Zweig told me about an interesting subject for a ballet— but it ranged just about from Prometheus to Nijinski, and was too much for me at sixty-eight. After that he suggested, shyly, the Ben Jonson subject, and I knew at once that this was my comic opera and grabbed it. In the summer, in Salzburg, he presented me with the idea for the entire play, which, in its blend of noble lyric poetry and farce constitutes an entirely new genre of *opera buffa*. In the autumn the text was done. Except for a minor cut in Act II (Morosus/Aminta) I was able to set it to music lock, stock, and barrel, without the slightest further change. None of my earlier operas was so easy to compose, or gave me such light-hearted pleasure. Then came the Third Reich, and with it his expulsion from the new Kultur state.

Everybody who read Zweig's text was enthusiastic about the witty, poetic, and truly dramatic book. The opera had already been accepted in Dresden when the anti-Semitic bomb burst in Bayreuth as a result of an attack by someone by the name of Will Vesper, writing in *Freiheitskampf*.

In the morning after my first performance of *Parsifal*, Minister Dr. Goebbels (after having said to Winifred Wagner the fateful words: "Little monk, you are on a difficult mission" *) entered

---

* Goebbels, evidently referring to himself on his way to beard the lion, was quoting Georg von Frundsberg, Landsknecht leader and head of Emperor

my room in "Wahnfried." I received him, saying it was perhaps significant that in the house of the "great martyr" I too, the smaller man, had to suffer my martyrdom. I told him that I did not wish to embarrass Adolf Hitler and himself by performing my opera, and that I was willing to withdraw *Die schweigsame Frau* altogether and to forego all showings at home and abroad. Goebbels said later that this talk had "deeply impressed" him— perhaps because I told him openly that the whole affair was a "big disgrace." In parting we agreed to submit the score to the Führer for a final decision. Before that Goebbels had commented that he was able to muzzle the press but was not able to prevent the throwing of a stink bomb at the opening night.

In the afternoon I returned to Garmisch. Next day Goebbels called up, saying that he had carefully considered my "case," had also talked with Hitler, and that he wanted me to submit the libretto. Goebbels added that if the book was unobjectionable (other than being authored by an uncomfortably talented Jew), he hoped that there would be no difficulties with the world premiere in Dresden.

And so it was. The work by itself won the victory, although Hitler and Goebbels did not attend the Dresden performance— either on purpose or, as was announced, prevented from flying by a storm in Hamburg.

State Commissioner Hinkel then gave a good, warm talk at the City Hall. It is a sad time when an artist of my rank has to ask a brat of a minister what he may set to music and what he may have performed. I, too, belong to the nation of "servants and waiters." ** I almost envy my friend Stefan Zweig, persecuted for his race, who now definitely refuses to work with me in public or in secret because, he says, he does not want to have any "special privileges" in the Third Reich. To be honest, I don't understand

---

Charles V's army. Frundsberg said these words to Martin Luther, when the latter was summoned to appear before the Diet of the Empire in Worms because of his teachings, 1521.

** Germans sometimes refer to themselves as the people of "Dichter und Denker" (poets and thinkers). The assonance "Diener und Kellner" (servants and waiters) may be a derogatory play on words.

this Jewish solidarity and regret that the "artist" Zweig cannot rise above "political fashions." If we do not preserve artistic freedom ourselves, how can we expect it from soap-box orators in taverns?

With *Die schweigsame Frau* my life's work definitely seems to have come to an end. Otherwise I might have been able to create other works not entirely without merit. It is regrettable.

July 3, 1935

Translator's Postscript

Richard Strauss, despite the intercepted letter of June 17, 1935, remained in Nazi Germany, where he conducted operas and concerts in the following years and throughout the war. After the war he moved to Switzerland, but in 1949 he returned to Garmisch, where he died, highly honored, on September 8, aged 85.

Stefan Zweig moved to England shortly before Hitler's takeover of Austria in 1938, later to the United States and to Brazil. His books were burned in Germany. Exhausted by years of homeless wandering and despairing at the world, he and his wife Elisabeth died on February 22, 1942, by their own hands. He was 60.

M. K.

Sächsische Staatstheater
Opernhaus

Montag, am 24. Juni 1935

Anfang **6** Uhr

Außer Anrecht

Uraufführung

Die schweigsame Frau

Komische Oper in drei Aufzügen

Frei nach Ben Jonson von Stefan Zweig

Musik von Richard Strauß

Musikalische Leitung: Karl Böhm   Inszenierung: Josef Gielen

Personen:

Sir Morosus		Friedrich Plaschke
Seine Haushälterin		Helene Jung
Der Barbier		Matthieu Ahlersmeyer
Henry Morosus		Martin Kremer
Aminta, seine Frau		Maria Cebotari
Isotta		Erna Sack
Carlotta	Komödianten	Marion Hundt
Vanuzzi		Kurt Böhme
Farfallo		Ludwig Ermold
Morbio		Rudolf Schmalnauer

Chor der Komödianten und Nachbarn

Ort der Handlung:

Zimmer des Sir Morosus in einem Vorort Londons

Zeit etwa 1780

Chöre: Karl Maria Pembaur / Tanz im dritten Akt: Werner Stammer

Bühnenbild: Adolf Mahnke   Einrichtung Georg Brandt   Trachten: Leonhard Santo

Pausen nach dem ersten und zweiten Akt

Krank: Liesel von Schuch, Hermann Kutzschbach, Horst Falke

Sämtliche Plätze müssen vor Beginn der Vorstellung eingenommen werden

Textbücher sind für 1,00 RM vormittags an der Kasse und abends bei den Türschließern zu haben

Gekaufte Karten werden nur bei Änderung der Vorstellung zurückgenommen

Einlaß 5¼ Uhr   Anfang 6 Uhr   Ende geg. 9¼ Uhr

Editor's Notes

1. Anton Kippenberg (1874–1950), Director of Insel-Verlag.

2. "A Letter by Wolfgang Amadeus Mozart to his Augsburg Cousin: Published and Reproduced for the First Time for Stefan Zweig in Salzburg, 1931." The private print contains a facsimile and the text of the letter dated October 5, 1777. Fifty copies were printed; copy No. 31 has the following dedication to Strauss from Zweig: "To Dr. Richard Strauss with devoted reverence. Stefan Zweig."

3. It is Mozart's last letter to his Augsburg cousin ("Vienne ce 21 d'octobre 1781"). This letter was in Strauss's house in Vienna (Jacquingasse 10) and disappeared in the turmoil of 1945.

4. See also Strauss's letter of May 25, 1916 and Hofmannsthal's reply of May 30, 1916 in *Briefwechsel: Richard Strauss/Hugo v. Hofmannsthal*, Zurich: Atlantis Verlag, 1952. [Translated as *The Correspondence between Richard Strauss and Hugo von Hofmannsthal* by Hanns Hammelmann and Ewald Osers, introduction by Edward Sackville-West, London: William Collins, 1961. Further references to the German edition are cited as *B:S/H.*]

5. *Die schweigsame Frau* [*The Silent Woman*]. The working title was "Sir Morosus." Stefan Zweig's libretto is based on the comedy *Epicoene* or *The Silent Woman* by Ben Jonson, English dramatist and poet (1573–1637). This comedy had been used before as the basis for the opera *Angiolina ossia Il Matrimonio* (composer Antonio Salieri, librettist C. P. Defranceschi, Vienna, 1800) and the opera *Lord Spleen* (composer Mark Lothar, librettist H. F. Koenigsgarten, Dresden, 1930). The great success of Zweig's free adaptation of Ben Jonson's *Volpone* caused Zweig to base once again the libretto Strauss requested on a Ben Jonson comedy. For *Volpone*, Zweig based his adaptation on a French summary by J. H. Jusserand (included in Jusserand's *Histoire littéraire du peuple anglais*); for *Die schweigsame Frau*, Zweig again did not use the original, but a German translation by Ludwig Tieck (transmitted to Zweig by Richard Friedenthal), included in the second part of *Poetisches Journal*, published 1800. The title there is *Epicoene, oder Das stumme Mädchen*. Tieck changed the title to *Epicoene, oder*

das stille Frauenzimmer in an adaptation prepared for the 12th volume of the collected works, published in 1829. For the history of *The Silent Woman* and its textual and musical adaptation by Stefan Zweig and Richard Strauss, see Alfred Mathis, "Stefan Zweig as Librettist and Richard Strauss," *Music & Letters*, XXV: 3 and 4 (July and October, 1944), London.

6. *Marie Antoinette.*

7. In early April Strauss gave concerts in Florence, Genoa, and Milan. In Milan, besides, *Elektra* was newly staged.

8. *Marie Antoinette.*

9. Strauss had conducted *Fidelio* on August 24 at the Salzburg Festival. He conducted a second performance August 26.

10. Berlin publisher.

11. At the end of November, Strauss had played [the piano part of] his sonata for violin and piano on the occasion of a Strauss celebration in Zurich, together with [Hungarian violinist] Stefi Geyer, and had conducted *Frau ohne Schatten.* On December 6 he was in Strasbourg.

12. Julius Korngold (1860–1945) was music critic of the *Neue Freie Presse*, Vienna.

13. A quotation from the third act of Wagner's *Meistersinger.* ["Bar" is a strophe in minnesong.]

14. Guy de Pourtales, *Richard Wagner: Mensch und Meister*, as translated from the French by Dr. Anton Mayer, published by Th. Knaur, Berlin (n.d.). Strauss did not write the requested foreword.

15. Hans Sassmann, *Dan Reich der Träumer: Kulturgeschichte Oesterreichs vom Urzustand bis zur Republik*, published by Amonesta, Berlin-Vienna, 1932.

16. Strauss ended the opera with Morosus' monologue.

17. The musical pasage is from Richard Strauss's song "Ich trage meine Minne," words by Karl Henckell, opus 32, number 1. In writing it down from memory Strauss made a few errors. The correct text reads:

Ja — dass ich dich ge- funden, du liebes

Kind, das freut mich alle Tage, die mir be-schie-den sind.

18. Strauss treated the mentioned passage as a trio—piano score pages 131–132—without adding the barber as a counterpoint; Zweig wrote a few verses of Aminta ("O herbe Schmach, o bittre Seligkeit") for it. The enclosure is not preserved.

19. Erich Engel.

20. Compare, in *B:S/H*, the letter of June 16, 1927 (Strauss) and of July 1, 1927 (Hofmannsthal).

21. Arnold Zweig (1887–1968), dramatist, novelist, essayist.

22. On March 28, 1933, the Nazi party ordered the boycott against Jews, which started on April 1.

23. *Arabella*. The world premiere, conducted by Clemens Krauss and with Viorica Ursuleac as Arabella, took place on July 1, 1933, at the Dresden opera.

24. The "Vienna version" of *Die aegyptische Helena* was first performed August 4, 1933, at the Salzburg Festival, conducted by Clemens Krauss. [The Dresden world premiere was in 1928.]

25. This refers perhaps to the orchestra score or the short score of the *Helena* changes.

26. Richard Strauss, without previous inquiry, was named president of the Reich Music Chamber on November 15, 1933. The inauguration of the Chamber was on February 13, 1934.

27. Richard Strauss's birthday, June 11, 1934.

28. *Calandria*, comedy by Bernardo Dovici da Bibiena (1470–1520).

29. Giovanni Battista Casti (1724–1830), librettist and rival of Lorenzo da Ponte. The title, *Prima la musica e poi le parole*, of his *divertimento teatrale* written to be performed in the imperial gardens of Schönbrunn (Vienna) and set to music by the Italian composer Antonio Salieri (1740–1825), provided the basic idea for the later *Capriccio* by Strauss-Krauss. See Stefan Zweig's letter of August 23, 1934 and thereafter.

30. The London premiere of *Arabella* (a guest performance of the Dresden Opera) took place May 17, 1934 (repeat performances May 21, 25, 29). Conducted by Clemens Krauss, directed by Otto Erhardt. Cast: Viorica Ursuleac (Arabella), Margit Bokor (Zdenka), Rut Berglund (Adelaide), Alfred Jerger (Mandryka), Josef Sterneck (Waldner), Martin Kremer (Matteo).

31. See *B:S/H*, the letters dated July 12, 1927 (Strauss) and July 16, 1927 (Hofmannsthal).

32. Strauss was forbidden to conduct *Fidelio* and an orchestra concert at the Salzburg Festival 1934. Only a few days before the performance of *Elektra*, conducted by Clemens Krauss, he could, at least, get permission to be present. As late as August 8 he had wired Krauss: "Will ask government again. Definitive decision expected tomorrow or day after

tomorrow. Sincere thanks and warm regards. Innocent and deeply saddened. Strauss."

33. Richard Strauss conducted Wagner's *Parsifal* at the Bayreuth Festival.

34. See note 31.

35. The future *Friedenstag*. The libretto, inspired by Calderon's *La redención de Breda*, was written by Joseph Gregor, who used the draft as described in this letter. See *Richard Strauss/Joseph Gregor, Briefwechsel 1934–1949*, ed. by Roland Tenschert (Salzburg: O. Müller, 1955); hereinafter cited as *B:S/G*.

36. From this idea developed the musical conversation piece *Capriccio*. For information on the close collaboration between Clemens Krauss and Strauss on this work, see W. Schuh, *Über Opern von Richard Strauss* (Zurich, 1947) and *B:S/G*.

37. *Maria Stuart*.

38. Published by Insel-Verlag, 1925.

39. *24. Oktober 1648* was the tentative title for *Friedenstag*.

40. The score for *Die schweigsame Frau* was concluded October 20, 1934.

41. At issue is a much-talked-about comment attributed to Toscanini: He would take off his hat for Strauss the composer, but put it back on again for Strauss the man.

42. In early November Strauss had conducted a symphony concert, *Ariadne*, and *Rosenkavalier*.

43. The score for the Potpourri Overture of *Die schweigsame Frau* carries the date of completion "Garmisch, January 17, 1935."

44. Zweig became acquainted, through Dr. Richard Friedenthal, with *La Celestina: Tragicomedia de Calisto y Melibea*, as translated by Eduard von Bülow; the first act is presumably by Rodrigo Cota, the following twenty acts by Fernando de Roja. Strauss was familiar, in addition to the verse adaptation by Richard Zoosmann recommended by Zweig, with Bülow's version, and referred to it when he corresponded about this material later with Joseph Gregor.

45. When Zweig agreed to work on *Die schweigsame Frau* for Strauss, he had asked for the draft of the piano score. It is today in the autograph collection of Zweig's estate. See illustration on page 34.

46. Strauss met Zweig's request by writing at the end of Act III: "Started October 1, 1932, completed October 20, 1934." The short score (see illustration on page 34) carries at the beginning the notation: "Started February 23, 1933." The Potpourri Overture says "Garmisch, January 17, 1935." The libretto of *Die schweigsame Frau* (Berlin: Adolph Fürstner) has no date.

47. See *B:S/H*, the letters dated April 27, 1906 (Hofmannsthal),

December 22, 1907 (Strauss), January 3, 1908 (Hofmannsthal), February 20, 1908 (Strauss), May 12, 1909 (Hofmannsthal), and September 31 (read October), 1910 (Hofmannsthal).

48. Alfred Kerr's scenes for *Peregrinus Proteus*, written 1920–1921, are included in S. Fischer's almanac *Das vierzigste Jahr*, published Berlin, 1926.

49. Joseph Gregor made a *Semiramis* draft for Strauss, which the composer rejected. But *Friedenstag* (originally *24. Oktober 1648*) was worked out and set to music. See the letters that follow. Besides this, Gregor wrote the libretti for *Daphne* and, using Hofmannsthal's *Danae* scenario, for *Die Liebe der Danae*. Strauss and Gregor met first on July 7, 1935, in Berchtesgaden.

50. For *Semiramis*.

51. See *B:S/G*. Gregor letter, dated May 3, 1935, p. 21.

52. Gregor mailed the *Semiramis* draft to Strauss on May 12, 1935. See *B:S/G*, p. 27.

53. Gregor's *Semiramis* draft. Strauss's answer to the draft is included in his letter to Gregor, dated May 24, 1935. See *B:S/G*, p. 28.

54. Strauss and Zweig did not meet until June 2, in Bregenz. See the letters dated May 27 and June 8, 1935.

55. The piano score and the libretto read: "Comic opera in three acts, freely adapted from Ben Jonson by Stefan Zweig."

56. "Timidia" was left standing (piano score, pages 235 and 286), also the other mentioned points.

57. Some excerpts from Strauss's notations were published, with the composer's agreement, shortly before his death, in *Betrachtungen und Erinnerungen*, edited by W. Schuh (Zurich and Freiburg: Atlantis Verlag, 1949).

58. The cast of the world premiere of *Die schweigsame Frau* (State Opera, Dresden, June 24, 1935) was as follows. Conductor: Dr. Karl Böhm; director: Josef Gielen: stage sets: Adolf Mahnke; Aminta: Maria Cebotari; Morosus: Friedrich Plaschke; Henry: Martin Kremer; Barber: Matthieu Ahlersmeyer.

59. This letter, addressed to Stefan Zweig's Zurich address (Hotel Bellerive) was intercepted by the Gestapo in Dresden and never reached its destination. The governor of Saxony, Martin Mutschmann, sent a photographic copy of it to Adolf Hitler, with the following cover letter:

The Governor of Saxony
My Führer!
The enclosed photocopy of a letter by Herr Dr. Strauss to the Jew Stefan Zweig fell into the hands of the Gestapo of Saxony; it is transmitted for your information.

I would like to add that the world premiere of *Die schweigsame Frau* took place before a full house, including five hundred invited guests; the second performance was so sparsely attended that the management issued free tickets; the third performance was canceled, purportedy because of illness of the principal actress.

Heil, respectfully,

Martin Mutschmann

Photocopy enclosed

In a memorandum dated July 10, 1935, Richard Strauss comments on the events resulting from the denunciation:

On July 6 Ministerial Counselor Keudell, commissioned by State Secretary Funk, called on me [in Berchtesgaden] and demanded that I resign as president of the Reich Music Chamber for reasons of 'ill health.' I did so at once.

Herr Keudell pointed several times to a red-marked copy of a personal letter to my friend and, up to now, collaborator St. Zweig. Although *the full name of the sender* appeared on the cover, the letter had apparently been opened by the state police of Saxony, and several (!) government offices in Berlin had been informed (*allegedly*; Dr. Frank thinks it's a fraud). I did not know that I, the president of the Reich Music Chamber, was under direct state police surveillance, and that I, after a life of creating eminent works 'recognized in the entire world' was not considered above criticism as 'a good German.' Yet, the unheard-of has happened: Herr Minister Goebbels dismissed me without even asking for an explanation of the sequestered letter, which, to unauthorized readers not aware of the background, and part of an involved correspondence concerned with purely artistic questions, is bound to be misunderstood.

The beginning of the letter about Zweig's Jewish stubbornness and his (understandable) feeling of solidarity with his persecuted tribal brethren contained the obvious answer that Teuton composers have never considered whether their compositions were sufficiently German and Aryan. We simply compose, ever since Bach, whatever our talent permits us, and we are Aryans and Germans without further being aware of it. This can hardly be construed as treason, but is loyal service to the fatherland, even though my libretto, like Mozart's, was written by a non-Aryan. About the passage most heavily marked in red, I may be in disagreement with Dr. Goebbels who, as a statesman, naturally has to judge people differently; the passage says that for me—it's a personal view, expressed in a personal letter—the 'people' start when they become the 'audience,' that is, people begin with the upper two million, the educated audience that paid their tickets in full—not those who for 15–30 pfennigs listen to *Meistersinger* or *Tristan*, causing great financial loss to the theaters and requiring ever larger subsidies from the government if the theaters are to fulfill truly higher cultural goals. Hence, this passage also concerns a purely artistic question, not a question of *my* purse, as it was evidently maliciously interpreted.

Following the entry of this memorandum, intended for the government, in his notebooks are other comments by Strauss including the following:

> Now I might examine the price I had to pay for not keeping away, from the beginning, from the National Socialist movement. It all started when, to do a favor to the Philharmonic Orchestra and upon the urging of Kopsch* and Rasch, I substituted in the last subscription concert for Bruno Walter who had been driven out. The honorarium of 1,500 marks I gave to the orchestra. That started a storm against me by the foreign and especially the Jewish Viennese press, which did more damage to me in the eyes of all decent people than the German government can ever compensate me for. I was slandered as a servile, selfish anti-Semite, whereas in truth I have always stressed at every opportunity to all the people that count here (much to my disadvantage) that I consider the Streicher-Goebbels Jew baiting as a disgrace to German honor, as evidence of incompetence, the basest weapon of untalented, lazy mediocrity against a higher intelligence and greater talent. I openly testify here that I have received so much support, so much self-sacrificing friendship, so much generous help and intellectual inspiration from Jews that it would be a crime not to acknowledge it all with gratitude.
>
> True, I had adversaries in the Jewish press; compared with them my relationship with my opposite pole Gustav Mahler could almost be called friendly. But my worst and most malicious enemies were "Aryans"—I merely need to mention the names of Perfall, Oscar Merz (*Münchener Neueste Nachrichten*), Theodor Göring (*Der Sammler*), Felix Mottl, Franz Schalk, Weingartner, and the whole party press: *Völkischer Beobachter* and the rest.

* Dr. Julius Kopsch (1887–1970), Berlin jurist, composer, and conductor; after the Second World War, he founded the International Richard Strauss Society in Berlin, which, after Kopsch's death, was reestablished in Vienna. Hugo Rasch, music editor of the *Völkischer Beobachter*, and an early member of the Nazi Storm Troopers, was mentioned in an earlier letter by Strauss as a friend.

In addition, Strauss's notes contain, under the date of February 7, 1937, the following comments referring to the controversial letter:

> Yesterday I learned that Dr. Goebbels is spreading the fairy tale that I wrote two letters in Dresden at the same time, one to the Reich Culture Chamber and one to Herr Stefan Zweig. Now they are scared of being accused of a cultural blunder and so they want to justify the illegal opening of my letter to Switzerland, its seizure by the Gestapo, and the denunciation—even by several ministries, according to Keudell!—by saying that *I mixed up the envelopes*, so that my letter to Zweig was sent directly to Goebbels!!!
>
> There is a second, still more stupid, version: that the mixup was engineered by me intentionally in order to let the Propaganda Ministry know in this way about my dissatisfaction—very funny. That would be just like me—as if I had not told Herr Goebbels my displeasure with the ways of the Theater Chamber at all times and directly!!!

The intercepted letter to Zweig, together with the denouncing Mutschmann letter to Hitler, were first published in the newspaper *Die Welt*, March 27, 1948.

60. Draft for *Prima la musica e poi le parole*.

61. Refers to a conflict between Richard Strauss and the Dresden Opera management about the suppression of Zweig's name. Because it is frequently said that at the world premiere of *Die schweigsame Frau* Stefan Zweig's name as librettist was suppressed and because Strauss is accused of tolerating this suppression in silence, let it be stated here that the program—shown on p. 112—shows Stefan Zweig's name. The events that preceded the world premiere are described by Friedrich von Schuch (the son of the conductor Ernst von Schuch) in *Richard Strauss, Ernst v. Schuch und Dresdens Oper*, published by VEB Verlag der Kunst, Dresden (in collaboration with Dresdner Verlag), on pages 133 ff. (no date), as follows:

> At the time I was the head of the administration of the state theaters and therefore representative of the general manager [Paul Adolph]. My boss who, after prolonged efforts, had obtained permission for the world premiere of the work, even though the libretto was by Stefan Zweig, decided that the librettist's name should not appear on the program. Incomprehensibly, however, he failed to have an understanding about this with Strauss, although, since we knew Strauss's mind well, we pointed out repeatedly (especially Fanto did) that a clarification was necessary.
>
> The authors gave the work the following title: "Die schweigsame

Frau, comic opera in three acts. Freely adapted from Ben Jonson by Stefan Zweig. Music by Richard Strauss." The general manager believed he could create a *fait accompli* and ordered, without informing Strauss, that the middle part of the title should read only: "From the English of Ben Jonson."

Two days before the world premiere in June [in the original erroneously "July"] 1935, Strauss, with Fanto and myself, sat in his room at the Hotel Bellevue playing his beloved Skat. Suddenly, to the shock of his partners, Strauss said out of the blue: "I want to see the program." Evidently he sensed some disaster. Now good counsel was needed. The general manager, after some resistance, agreed by telephone to let Strauss see the printer's proof of the program. I let dinner pass, and then in the hotel lobby presented the proof that had meanwhile been brought there. Strauss got his well-known flushed face and declared: "You can do this but I will leave tomorrow and the show can take place without me." Then, by his own hands, he restored the official wording of the program. The next day a conference took place in the Staatskanzlei, at which neither Strauss nor I were present. The result was compliance with Strauss's wishes. . . . *Die schweigsame Frau*, a delightful performance with Maria Cebotari and Friedrich Plaschke, conducted by Karl Böhm, had to be dropped from the repertory after three performances, and thus from the German stage.

Schuch's book also cites a letter from Richard Strauss to Joseph Keilberth, conductor of the first postwar performance of *Die schweigsame Frau* in Dresden, referring to the episode (page 138).

Baden near Zurich

October 12, 1946

. . . so now, after ten [correctly: eleven] years the honorable Sir Morosus has been liberated from the concentration camp of the Reich Theater Chamber and been brought back to his birthplace, where twelve [correctly: eleven] years ago I had great trouble getting the name of the librettist on the program.

62. Leonhard Fanto, for forty years stage designer of the Dresden state theaters (he died 1940 in Grainau) wrote to Richard Strauss from Karlsbad on July 9, 1934: "I received a detailed letter from Stefan Zweig with suggestions for the stage setting of *Die schweigsame Frau*. He envisions the England during the trading era, that is, the reign of George III. Thomas Rowlandson and Gillray have beautifully portrayed that time in their delightful graphics. Rowlandson's 'Vauxhall Gardens' gives you a vivid picture of the costumes of that era, which has hardly

ever been shown on the stage. Please drop me a line to say that you approve." The libretto of *Die schweigsame Frau* originally carried the notation: "Time: approximately 1760." This figure was pasted over with the notation "Time: approximately 1780." The score and the piano score say "Time: approximately 1760."

63. Because of the suppression of the opera, the guest performance did not take place. Neither Goebbels nor Hitler attended the world premiere.

64. This Zweig letter is not extant.

65. Imprecise quotation from the ending of Act II of *Die schweigsame Frau*. (Barber: "Get going, then, don't hesitate.")

66. See note 49.

67. See *B:S/G*, Strauss's letter dated September 25, 1935.

68. Stefan Zweig had queried Felix von Weingartner, then director of the Vienna Opera, about a performance of *Die schweigsame Frau* on that stage. See *B:S/G*, letters dated December 24, 1935, December 27, 1935, and January 1, 1936. Strauss's communication with Zweig, mentioned in the last of these letters, is no longer extant.

69. Dr. Erwin Kerber, counselor in the Ministry of Education in Vienna, succeeded Weingartner on September 1, 1936 (till September 1, 1940) as director of the Vienna State Opera.

70. The opening evening, arranged by the Vienna Richard Strauss Society on December 15, 1935 (repeated January 10, 1936), took place in the auditorium of the Vienna Women's Club, with Stefan Zweig attending. The cast included: Dr. Ernst Bachrich (piano), Antburg (Aminta), Braun-Fernwald (housekeeper), Rochmis (Morosus), Köhler (barber), and Nagel (Henry). The introductory address was given by Dr. Willi Reich. Information from Dr. Roland Tenschert, Vienna.)